System-Level Modeling and Design Space Exploration for Multiprocessor Embedded System-on-Chip Architectures

ACADEMISCH PROEFSCHRIFT

ter verkrijging van de graad van doctor
aan de Universiteit van Amsterdam,
op gezag van Rector Magnificus,
prof. mr. P. F. van der Heijden
ten overstaan van een door het College voor Promoties ingestelde
commissie, in het openbaar te verdedigen in de Aula der Universiteit
op donderdag 30 november 2006, te 13.00 uur

door

Çağkan Erbaş

geboren te Kütahya, Turkije

Promotiecommissie:

Promotor:	prof. dr. C. Jesshope
Co-promotor:	dr. A.D. Pimentel
Overige leden:	prof. drs. M. Boasson
	dr. A.C.J. Kienhuis
	prof. dr. L. Thiele
	prof. dr. S. Vassiliadis

Faculteit der Natuurwetenschappen, Wiskunde en Informatica

The work described in this thesis has been carried out in the ASCI graduate school and was financially supported by PROGRESS, the embedded systems research program of the Dutch organization for Scientific Research NWO, the Dutch Ministry of Economic Affairs and the Technology Foundation STW.

ASCI dissertation series number 132.

System-Level Modeling and Design Space Exploration for Multiprocessor Embedded System-on-Chip Architectures

Cover design: René Staelenberg, Amsterdam
Cover illustration: “Binary exploration” by Çağkan Erbaş

NUR 980
ISBN 90-5629-455-5
ISBN-13 978-90-5629-455-7

Acknowledgments

Over the last four years that I have been working towards my PhD degree, I had the opportunity to meet and co-operate with many bright people. I am very indebted to these people, without their support and guidance I would not be able to make my accomplishments come true.

First, I would like to thank my daily supervisor and co-promotor Andy. I am grateful to you for the excellent working environment you have provided by being a very sensible person and manager, for your confidence in me from the very beginning, for giving as much freedom as I asked for doing my research, for reading everything I had written down even they sometimes included formal and boring stuff, and finally for all the good words and motivation while we were tackling various difficult tasks. Working with you has always been inspiring and fun for me.

From my very first day at the University of Amsterdam, Simon has been my roommate, colleague, and more importantly my friend. I want to thank you for helping me by answering numerous questions I had over research, Dutch bureaucracy, housing market, politics, and life in general. Mark, who joined us a little later, has also become a very good friend. Thanks for both of you guys for making our room a nice place to work. We should still get rid of the plant, though!

The official language during the lunch break was Dutch. Well, I guess, I did my best to join the conversations. Of course, all the important stuff that you don't want to miss like football, playstation, cars, women were being discussed during the lunch. So, learning Dutch has always been essential and I am still in progress. I must mention Edwin and Frank as our official lunch partners here.

Here I also would like to thank my promotor Chris for his interest and support to our research. All members of the computer systems architecture group definitely deserve to be acknowledged here. These are Peter, Konstantinos, Zhang, Thomas, Liang and Tessa. Thanks for all of you! I will not forget the delicious birthday cakes we have eaten together.

I have been a member of the Artemis project which was a PROGRESS/STW funded project with various partners. I must mention Stamatis Vassiliadis and Georgi Kuzmanov from Delft University of Technology; Todor Stefanov, Hristo Nikolov, Bart Kienhuis, and Ed Deprettere from Leiden University. I am further grateful to Stamatis and Bart, together with Maarten Boasson from University of Amsterdam and Lothar Thiele from ETH Zürich for reading my thesis and taking part in my promotion committee.

Luckily, there were other Turkish friends in the computer science department.

This made my life here in Amsterdam more enjoyable. Hakan, Ersin, Başak, Özgül, and Gökhan, I will be very much missing our holy coffee breaks in the mornings. Thank you all for your company!

The following people from our administrative department helped me to resolve various bureaucratic issues. I am thankful to Dorien Bisselink, Erik Hitipeuw, Han Habets, and Marianne Roos.

I was a very lucky person born to an outstanding family. I owe a lot to my parents and grandparents who raised me with great care and love. Today, I am still doing my best to deserve their confidence and belief in me.

And finally my dear wife Selin. Since we met back in 1997, you have always been a very supportive and caring person. You never complained once when we had to live apart, or study during the nights and weekends. You have always been patient with me and I really appreciate it.

Çağkan Erbaş
October 2006
Amsterdam

To the memory of my grandfather Alaettin Öğüt (1928–2004).

Contents

1

Introduction

Modern embedded systems come with contradictory design constraints. On one hand, these systems often target mass production and battery-based devices, and therefore should be cheap and power efficient. On the other hand, they still need to show high (sometimes real-time) performance, and often support multiple applications and standards which requires high programmability. This wide spectrum of design requirements leads to complex heterogeneous System-on-Chip (SoC) architectures – consisting of several types of processors from fully programmable microprocessors to configurable processing cores and customized hardware components, integrated on a single chip. These multiprocessor SoCs have now become the keystones in the development of late embedded systems, devices such as digital televisions, game consoles, car audio/navigation systems, and 3G mobile phones.

The sheer architectural complexity of SoC-based embedded systems, as well as their conflicting design requirements regarding good performance, high flexibility, low power consumption and cost greatly complicate the system design. It is now widely believed that traditional design methods come short for designing these systems due to following reasons [79]:

- Classical design methods typically start from a single application specification, making them inflexible for broader exercise.
- Common evaluation practice still makes use of detailed cycle-accurate simulators for early design space exploration. Building these detailed simulation models requires significant effort, making them impractical in the early design stages. What is more, these low level simulators suffer from low simulation speeds which hinder fast exploration.

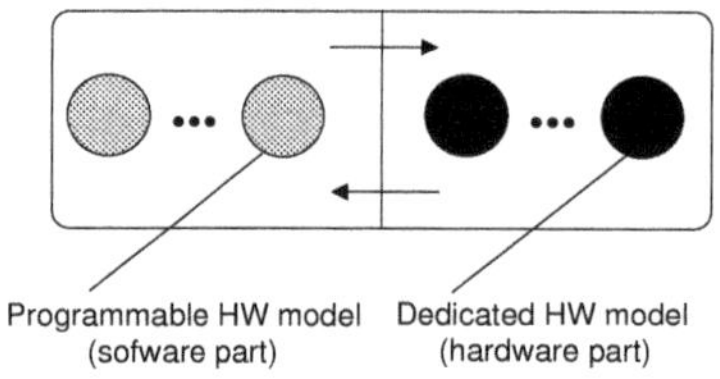

(a) Traditional hardware/software co-simulation.

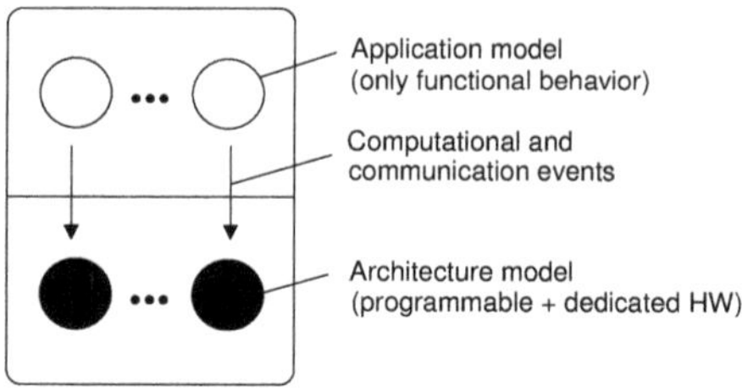

(b) The Artemis methodology separating application and architecture.

Figure 1.1: Embedded systems design methodologies.

Classical hardware/software (HW/SW) co-design methods typically start from a single system specification that is gradually refined and synthesized into an architecture implementation which consists of programmable (such as different kinds of processors) and/or dedicated components (i.e. ASICs). However, the major disadvantage of this approach is that it forces the designer to make early decisions on the HW/SW partitioning of the system – that is to identify parts of the system which will be implemented in hardware and software. The latter follows from the fact that the classical approach makes an explicit distinction between hardware and software models, which should be known in advance before a system can be built. The co-simulation frameworks that model the classical HW/SW co-design approach, generally combine two (rather low-level) simulators, one for simulating the programmable components running the software and one for the dedicated hardware. This situation is depicted in Figure 1.1(a). The common practice is to employ instruction-level simulators for the software part, while the hardware part is usually simulated using VHDL or Verilog. The grey (black) circles in Figure 1.1(a) represent software (hardware) components which are executed on programmable (dedicated) components, while the arrows represent the interactions between hardware and software simulators. The hardware and software simulators may run apart from each other [24], [58], [10], or they may also be integrated to form a monolithic simulator [86], [4], [49].

The Y-chart methodology [4], [56], which is followed in this thesis[1] and also in most recent work [65], [110], [70], [5] tries to improve the shortcomings of the classical approach by i) abandoning the usage of low-level (instruction-level or cycle-accurate) simulators for the early design space exploration (DSE), as such detailed simulators require considerable effort to build and suffer from low simulation speeds for effective DSE, and ii) abandoning a single system specification to describe both hardware and software. As illustrated in Figure 1.1(b), DSE frameworks following the Y-chart methodology recognize a clear separation between an *application model*, an *architecture model* and an explicit *mapping step* to relate the

[1]The Y-chart methodology was adopted by the Sesame framework of the Artemis project, in which the work described in this thesis was performed.

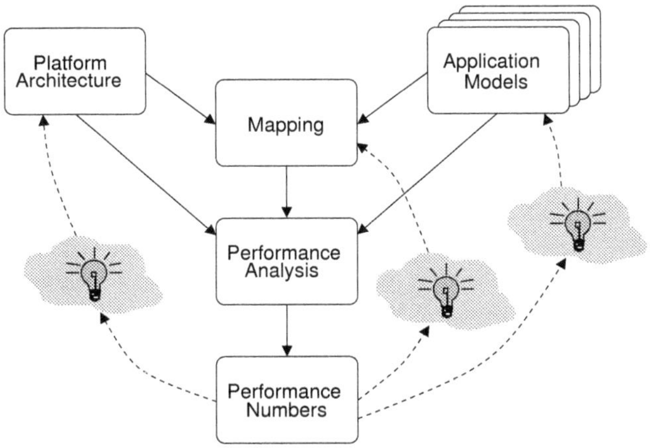

Figure 1.2: Y-chart approach for system evaluation.

application model to the architecture model. The application model describes the functional behavior of an application, independent of architectural specifics like the HW/SW partitioning or timing characteristics. When executed, the application model may, for example, emit application events (for both computation and communication) in order to drive the architectural simulation. The architecture model, which defines architecture resources and captures their timing characteristics, can simulate the performance consequences of the application events for both software (programmable components) and hardware (reconfigurable/dedicated) executions. Thus, unlike the traditional approach in which hardware and software simulation are regarded as the co-operating parts, the Y-chart approach distinguishes application and architecture simulation where the latter involves simulation of programmable as well as reconfigurable/dedicated parts.

The general design scheme with respect to the Y-chart approach is given in Figure 1.2. The set of application models in the upper right corner of Figure 1.2 drives the architecture design. As the first step, the designer studies these applications, makes some initial calculations, and proposes a candidate platform architecture. The designer then evaluates and compares several instances of the platform by mapping each application onto the platform architecture by means of performance analysis. The resulting performance numbers may inspire the designer to improve the architecture, restructure the application, or change the mapping. The possible designer actions are shown with the light bulbs in Figure 1.2. Decoupling application and architecture models allows designers to use a single application model to exercise different HW/SW partitionings and map it onto a range of architecture models, possibly representing different instances of a single platform or the same platform instance at various abstraction levels. This capability clearly demonstrates the strength of decoupling application and architecture models, fostering the reuse of both model types.

In order to overcome the aforementioned shortcomings of the classical HW/SW co-design, embedded systems design community has recently come up with a new design concept called *system-level design*, which incorporates ideas from the Y-chart approach, as well as the following new notions:

- *Early exploration of the design space.* In system-level design, designers start modeling and performance evaluation early in the design stage. System-level models, which represent application behavior, architecture characteristics, and the relation between application and architecture (issues such as mapping, HW/SW partitioning), can provide initial estimations on the performance [78], [5], power consumption [89], or cost of the design [52]. What is more, they do so at a high level of abstraction, and hence minimize the effort in model construction and foster fast system evaluation by achieving high simulation speeds. Figure 1.3 shows several abstraction levels that a system designer is likely to traverse in the way to the final implementation. After making some initial calculations, the designer proposes some candidate implementations. Each system-level implementation is then evaluated and compared at a high-level of abstraction one after another until a number of promising candidate implementations are identified. Because building these system-level models is relatively fast, the designer can repeat this process to cover a large design space. After this point, the designer further lowers the abstraction level, constructs cycle-accurate or synthesizable register transfer level (RTL) models, and hopefully reaches an optimal implementation with respect to his design criteria. This stepwise exploration of the design space requires an environment, in which there exist a number of models at different abstraction levels for the very same design. While the abstract executable models efficiently explore the large design space, more detailed models at the later stages convey more implementation details and subsequently attain better accuracy.

- *Platform architectures.* Platform-based design [55] is gaining popularity due to high chip design and manufacturing costs together with increasing time-to-market pressure. In this approach, a common platform architecture is specified and shared across multiple applications in a given application domain. This platform architecture ideally comes with a set of methods and tools which assists designers in the process of programming and evaluating such platform architectures. Briefly, platform-based design promotes the reuse of Intellectual Property (IP) blocks for the purpose of increasing productivity and reducing manufacturing costs by guaranteed high production volumes.

- *Separation of concerns.* Separating various aspects of a design allows for more effective exploration of alternative implementations. One fundamental separation in the design process, which is proposed by the Y-chart approach, is the isolation of application (i.e. *behavior*, what the system is supposed to do) and architecture (how it does it) [4], [56]. Another such separation is usually done between computation and communication. The latter, for example, can be realized at the application level by choosing an appropriate model of computation (MoC) for behavioral specification [64]. For example,

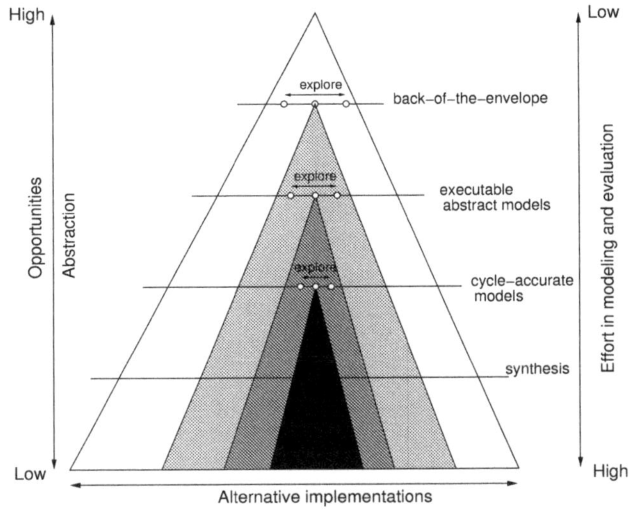

Figure 1.3: Abstraction pyramid showing different abstraction levels in system design. Models at the top are more abstract and require relatively less effort to build. Reversely, models at the bottom incorporate more details and are more difficult to build.

applications specified as Kahn process networks provide to a large extent such a separation where computation and communication are represented by the Kahn processes and the FIFO channels between them, respectively.

1.1 Related work in system-level design

Over the last decade or so, various system-level design environments have been developed both in academia and industry. In this section, we summarize a number of these system-level frameworks. We should note that the mentioned frameworks are selective rather than exhaustive. For example, earlier environments that are no longer in active development such as Polis [4] and VCC [101] are not included here. We start with the academical work.

Artemis [79], [76] is composed of mainly two system-level modeling and simulation environments, which have been utilized successively to explore the design space of multiprocessor system-on-chip (SoC) architectures. Many initial design principles (Y-chart based design, trace-driven co-simulation) from the Spade environment have been adopted and further extended (multiobjective search, architectural refinement, mixed-level simulation) by the Sesame environment.

Spade [67] is a trace-driven system-level co-simulation environment which emphasizes simplicity, flexibility, and easy interfacing to more detailed simulators. It provides a small library of architecture model components such as a black-box model of a processor, a generic bus model, a generic memory model, and a number of interfaces for connecting these components. Spade's architecture model components are implemented using a Philips in-house simulation environment called TSS (Tool for System Simulation), which is normally used to build cycle-accurate architecture simulators.

Sesame [23], [39] employs a small but powerful discrete-event simulation language called Pearl (see Chapter 2) to implement its architecture models. In addition to Y-chart based modeling and trace-driven system-level co-simulation which it inherits from Spade, the Sesame environment has additional capabilities such as pruning the design space by multiobjective search (Chapter 3), gradual model refinement (Chapter 4), and mixed-level modeling and simulation through coupling low-level simulators (Chapter 5). We leave further details of the Sesame environment to Chapter 2.

The **Archer** [110] project has also used the Spade environment for exploring the design space of streaming multiprocessor architectures. However, trace-driven co-simulation technique in Spade has been improved by making use of additional control constructs called symbolic programs. The latter allows to carry control information from the application model down to the architecture model.

Ptolemy [33] is an environment for simulation and prototyping of heterogeneous systems. It supports multiple MoC within a single system simulation. It does so by supporting domains to build subsystems each conforming to a different MoC. Using techniques such as hierarchical composition and refinement, the designer can specify heterogeneous systems consisting of various MoCs to model and simulate applications and architectures at multiple levels of abstraction. Ptolemy supports an increasing set of MoCs, including all dataflow MoCs [63]: Synchronous dataflow [62], Dynamic dataflow [15], (Kahn) process networks [54], as well as, finite state machines, discrete-event and continuous-time domains.

Metropolis [5] targets at integrating modeling, simulation, synthesis, and verification tools within a single framework. It makes use of the concept *metamodel*, which is a representation of concurrent objects which communicate through media. Internally, objects take actions sequentially. Nondeterministic behavior can be modeled and the set of possible executions are restricted by the metamodel constraints which represent in abstract form requirements assumed to be satisfied by the rest of the system. Architecture building blocks are driven by events which are annotated with the costs of interest such as the energy or time for execution. The mapping between functional and architecture models is established by a third network which also correlates the two models by synchronizing events between them.

Mescal [47] aims at the heterogeneous, application-specific, programmable multiprocessor design. It is based on an architecture description language. On the application side, the programmer should be able to use a combination of MoCs which is best suited for the application domain, whereas on the architecture side, an efficient mapping between application and architecture is to be achieved by making use of a correct-by-construction design path.

MILAN [70] is a hierarchical design space exploration framework which integrates a set of simulators at different levels of abstraction. At the highest level, it makes use of a performance estimator which prunes the design space by constraint satisfaction. Simulators range from high-level system simulators to cycle-accurate ISS simulators such as SimpleScalar [3]. Functional simulators, such as Matlab and SystemC, verify the application behavior. MILAN trades off between accuracy of the results and simulation speed by choosing from a range simulators at multiple abstraction levels. A feedback path from low-level simulations to refine high-level model parameters is also planned in the future.

GRACE++ [60] is a SystemC-based simulation environment for Network-on-Chip (NoC) centric multiprocessor SoC platform exploration. In GRACE++, there are two kinds (master and slave) of modules which can participate in a communication. Master modules can actively initiate transactions, while slave modules can only react passively. Typical master modules are processors, bus controllers, or ASIC blocks, whereas typical slave modules are memories or co-processors. On-chip communication services are provided by a generalized master interface. The processing of communication is handled by the NoC channel, which constitutes the central module of the simulation framework.

MESH [75] is a thread-based exploration framework which models systems using event sequences, where threads are ordered set of events with the tags of the events showing the ordering. Hardware building blocks, software running on programmable components, and schedulers are viewed as different abstraction levels that are modeled by software threads in MESH. Threads representing hardware elements are periodically activated, whereas software and scheduler threads have no guaranteed activation patterns. The main design parameter is a time budget which defines the hardware requirements of a software thread. Software time budgets are estimated by profiling beforehand, and used by the scheduler threads during simulation. The periodically activated hardware threads synchronize with the global system clock, while the scheduler threads allocates the available time budgets (i.e. hardware resources) to the software thread requirements.

EXPO [96] is an analytical exploration framework targeting the domain of network processor architectures. EXPO uses an abstract task graph for application description, where a task sequence is defined for each traffic flow. The architecture components are composed of processing cores, memories, and buses. Worst case service curves are associated with the architecture components, which represent the architectural resources. Mapping information is supplied with the scheduling policy for the architecture components. Non-linear arrival curves, which represent the worst-case behavior under all possible traffic patterns, model the workload imposed on the architecture. Multiobjective search algorithms are generally employed to solve the high-level synthesis problem under objectives such as the throughput values for different traffic scenarios and the total cost of the allocated resources. The total memory requirement of the implementation can become a problem constraint.

SymTA/S [48] is a formal DSE framework based on event streams. In SymTA/S, tasks in the application model are activated by the activation events which are triggered in accordance with one of the supported event models such as the *strictly periodic*, *periodic with jitter*, or the *sporadic* event model. Unlike the aforementioned environments, SymTA/S follows an interactive, designer-controlled approach where the designer can guide the search towards those sub-spaces which are considered to be worthy for further exploration.

When we look at the commercial tools, we see that many tools support SystemC as the common modeling and simulation language which allows to couple evaluation tools and applications written in C/C++ from different vendors. These tools typically model and evaluate systems at high abstraction levels, using various application and architecture model descriptions. We list two of these tools here, whereas up to date complete list can be found at the website of the SystemC Community [93].

CoWare Model Designer is a SystemC-based modeling and simulation environment for capturing complex IP blocks and verifying them. It supports transaction level modeling (TLM) [17] which is a discrete-event MoC employed to model the interaction between hardware and software components and the shared bus communication between them. In TLM, computational modules communicate through sending/receiving transactions, which is usually implemented as a high-level message passing communication protocol, while the modules themselves can be implemented at different levels of abstraction. Model Designer supports SystemC TLM model creation and simulations. It can further be coupled with third party tools for RTL-level implementation and verification.

Synopsys System Studio is another SystemC-based modeling and simulation tool which fully supports all abstraction levels and MoCs defined within the SystemC language. Model refinements down to RTL-level can be accomplished by incorporating cycle-accurate and bit true SystemC models. Hardware synthesis from SystemC is also supported by automatic Verilog generation. System Studio does not support an explicit mapping step from application to architecture. Instead, the designer implicitly takes these decisions while refining and connecting various SystemC models along his modeling and co-simulation path down to RTL-level.

1.2 Organization and contributions of this thesis

We address the design space exploration of multiprocessor system-on-chip (SoC) architectures in this thesis. More specifically, we strive to develop algorithms, methods, and tools to deal with a number of fundamental design problems which are encountered by the designers in the early design stages. The main contributions of this thesis are

- presentation of a new software framework (Sesame) for modeling and simulating embedded systems architectures at multiple levels of abstraction. The Sesame software framework implements some widely accepted ideas proposed by the embedded systems community such as Y-chart based design and trace-driven co-simulation, as well as several new ideas like the gradual model refinement and high-level model calibration which are still in early stages of development.

- derivation of an analytical model to capture early design decisions during the mapping stage in Sesame. The model takes into account three design objectives, and is solved to prune the large design space during the early stages of design. The promising architectures, which are identified by solving (instances of) the mathematical model using multiobjective optimizers, are further simulated by the Sesame framework for performance evaluation and validation. The experiments conducted on two multimedia applications reveal that effective and efficient design space pruning and exploration can be achieved by combining analytical modeling with system-level simulation.

- implementation of a new mapping strategy within Sesame which allows us to refine (parts of) system-level performance models. Our aim here is to increase evaluation accuracy by gradually incorporating more implementation details into abstract high-level models. The proposed refinement method also enables us to realize mixed-level co-simulations, where for example, one architecture model component can be modeled and simulated at a lower level of abstraction while the rest of the architecture components are still implemented at a higher level of abstraction.

- illustration of the practical application of design space pruning, exploration, and model refinement techniques proposed in this thesis. For this purpose, we traverse the complete design path of a multimedia application that is mapped on a platform architecture. Furthermore, we also show how system-level model calibration and validation can be realized by making use of additional tool-sets from the Artemis project in conjunction with Sesame.

- derivation of a new scheduling test condition for static priority schedulers of real-time embedded systems. The practical applicability of the derived condition is shown with experiments, where a number of task systems are shown to be schedulable on a uniprocessor system.

To name a few keywords related to the work performed in this thesis: *system-level modeling and simulation*, *platform-based design*, *design space pruning and exploration*, *gradual model refinement*, *model calibration*, *model validation*, *real-time behavior* and so on. Here is an outline of chapters.

Chapter 2 introduces our *system-level modeling and simulation* environment Sesame. We first introduce some key concepts employed within the Sesame framework such as the Y-chart approach and the trace-driven co-simulation technique. Then, we give a conceptual view of the Sesame framework, where we discuss its three layer structure in detail. This is followed by a section on the implementation details, in which we discuss Sesame's model description language YML and its application and architecture simulators. We conclude this chapter by presenting two techniques for calibrating system-level performance models.

Chapter 3 is dedicated to *design space pruning and exploration*. In Sesame, we employ analytical modeling/multiobjective search in conjunction with system-level modeling and simulation to achieve fast and accurate design space exploration. The chapter starts with introducing the analytical model for pruning the design space, and then continues with introducing exact and heuristic methods for multiobjective optimization together with metrics for performance comparisons. We conclude this chapter with experiments where we prune and explore the design space of two multimedia applications.

In Chapter 4, we develop a new methodology for *gradual model refinement* which is realized within a new mapping strategy. We first define event traces and their transformations which form the basis of the model refinements in this chapter. Then, we introduce the new mapping strategy, which is followed by a discussion of the dataflow actors and networks that implement the aforementioned model refinement. The chapter ends with an illustrative experiment.

Chapter 5 presents two case studies with a multimedia application where we make use of all methods and tools from Chapters 2, 3, and 4. In the first case study, we focus on the Sesame framework to illustrate how we prune and explore the design space of an M-JPEG encoder which is mapped onto a platform SoC architecture. Subsequently, we further refine one of the processing cores in the SoC platform using our dataflow-based method for model refinement. In the second case study, besides Sesame, we make use of other tool-sets from the Artemis project which allows us to perform system-level *model calibration and validation*.

Chapter 6 focuses on *real-time issues*. We first introduce a new task model which can model conditional code executions (such as if-then-else statements) residing in coarse-grained application processes. Then, we will derive a scheduling condition for static priority schedulers to schedule these tasks in a uniprocessor system. This is followed by a summary of previous work on dynamic schedulers. The chapter is concluded with an experimental section to illustrate the practical value of the derived static priority condition, where a number of task systems are shown to be schedulable under a given static priority assignment. The priority assignment satisfying the condition is located by a simulated annealing search framework.

Finally in Chapter 7, we first look back and summarize what we have achieved, and then look ahead to outline what can be accomplished next.

2

The Sesame environment

Within the context of the Artemis project [79], [76], we have been developing the Sesame framework [23], [78] for the efficient system-level performance evaluation and architecture exploration of heterogeneous embedded systems targeting the multimedia application domain. Sesame attempts to accomplish this by providing high-level modeling, estimation and simulation tools. Using Sesame a designer can construct system-level performance models, map applications onto these models with the help of analytical modeling and multiobjective optimization, explore their design space through high-level system simulations, and gradually lower the abstraction level in the system-level models by incorporating more implementation details into them in order to attain higher accuracy in performance evaluations.

The traditional practice for system-level performance evaluation through co-simulation often combines two types of simulators, one for simulating the programmable components running the software and one for the dedicated hardware part. For simulating the software part, low-level (instruction-level or cycle-accurate) simulators are commonly used. The hardware parts are usually simulated using hardware RTL descriptions realized in VHDL or Verilog. However, the drawbacks of such a co-simulation environment are i) it requires too much effort to build them, ii) they are often too slow for exploration, iii) they are inflexible in evaluating different hardware/software partitionings. Because an explicit distinction is made between hardware and software simulation, a complete new system is required for the assessment of each partitioning. To overcome these shortcomings, in accordance with the separation of concerns principle from Chapter 1, Sesame decouples application from architecture by recognizing two distinct models for them. For

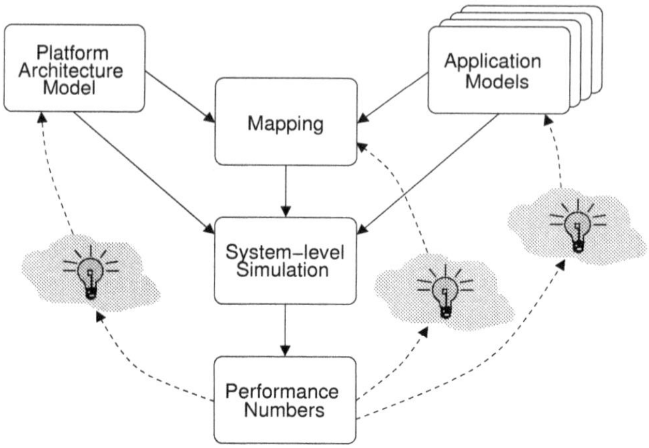

Figure 2.1: Y-Chart approach.

system-level performance evaluation, Sesame closely follows the Y-chart design methodology [4], [56] which is depicted in Figure 2.1. According to the Y-chart approach, an application model – derived from a target application domain – describes the functional behavior of an application in an architecture-independent manner. The application model is often used to study a target application and obtain rough estimations of its performance needs, for example to identify computationally expensive tasks. This model correctly expresses the functional behavior, but is free from architectural issues, such as timing characteristics, resource utilization or bandwidth constraints. Next, a platform architecture model – defined with the application domain in mind – defines architecture resources and captures their performance constraints. Finally, an explicit *mapping step* maps an application model onto an architecture model for co-simulation, after which the system performance can be evaluated quantitatively. The light bulbs in Figure 2.1 indicate that the performance results may inspire the system designer to improve the architecture, modify the application, or change the projected mapping. Hence, Y-chart modeling methodology relies on independent application and architecture models in order to promote reuse of both simulation models to the conceivable largest extent.

However, the major drawback of any simulation based approach, be it system-level or lower, in the early performance evaluation of embedded systems is their inability of covering the large design space. Because each simulation evaluates only one design point at a time, it does not matter how fast a system-level simulation is, it would still fail to examine many points in the design space. Analytical methods may be of great help here, as they can provide the designer with a small set of promising candidate points which can be evaluated by system-level simulation. This process is called *design space pruning*. For this purpose, we have developed a mathematical model to capture the trade-offs faced during the mapping stage in Sesame. Because the application to architecture mappings increase exponentially with the problem size, it is very important that effective steering is provided to the system designer which enables him to focus only on the promising mappings. The discussion on design space pruning is continued in Section 2.6, and more elaborately in Chapter 3 which is solely dedicated on this issue.

Furthermore, we support *gradual model refinement* in Sesame [77], [40]. As the designer moves down in the abstraction pyramid, the architecture model components start to incorporate more and more implementation details. This calls for a good methodology which enables architecture exploration at multiple levels of abstraction. Once again, it is essential in this methodology that an application model remains independent from architecture issues such as hardware/software partitioning and timing properties. This enables maintaining high-level and architecture-independent application specifications that can be reused in the exploration cycle. For example, designers can make use of a single application model to exercise different hardware-software partitionings or to map it onto different architecture models, possibly representing the same system architecture at various abstraction levels in the case of gradual model refinement. Ideally, these gradual model refinements should bring an abstract architecture model closer to the level of detail where it is possible to synthesize an implementation. In Sesame, we have proposed a refinement method [38] which is based on trace transformations and the dataflow implementations of these transformations within the co-simulation environment. The latter allows us to tackle the refinement issue at the architecture level, and thus preserves architecture-independent application models. Hence, model refinement does not hinder the reusability of application models. The elaborate discussion on architecture model refinement in Sesame is the subject of Chapter 4.

The remaining part of this chapter is dedicated to our modeling and simulation environment Sesame. We first discuss a technique used for co-simulation of application and architecture models, and subsequently discuss Sesame's infrastructure, which contains three layers, in detail. Next we proceed with discussing some of the related issues we find important, such as the software perspective of Sesame, mapping decision support for Sesame, and methods for obtaining more accurate numbers to calibrate the timing behavior of our high-level architecture model components. We finally conclude this chapter with a general summary and overview.

2.1 Trace-driven co-simulation

Exploration environments making a distinction between application and architecture modeling need an explicit mapping step to relate these models for co-simulation. In Sesame, we apply a technique called *trace-driven co-simulation* to carry out this task [79], [67]. In this technique, we first unveil the inherent task-level parallelism and inter-task communication by restructuring the application as a network of parallel communicating processes, which is called an *application model*. When the application model is executed, as will be explained later on, each process generates its own trace of events which represent the application workload imposed on the architecture by that specific process. These events are coarse-grained computation and communication operations such as *read(pixel-block,channel-id)*, *write(frame-header,channel-id)* or *execute(DCT)*. This approach may seem close to the classical trace-driven simulations used in general purpose processor design, for example to analyze memory hierarchies [99]. However, the classical approach typically uses fine-grained instruction-level operations and differs from our approach in this perspective.

The architecture models, on the other hand, simulate the performance consequences of the generated application events. As the complete functional behavior is already comprised in the application models, the generated event traces correctly reflect data-dependent behavior for particular input data. Therefore, the architecture models, driven by the application traces, only need to account for the performance consequences, i.e. timing behavior, and not for the functional behavior.

As already mentioned in Chapter 1, similar to Sesame, both the Spade [65] and Archer [110] environments make use of trace-driven co-simulation for performance evaluation. However, each of these environments uses its own architecture simulator and follows a different mapping strategy for co-simulation. For example, Archer uses symbolic programs (SPs), which are more abstract representations of Control Flow Data Flow Graphs (CDFGs), in its mapping layer. The SPs contain control structures like CDFGs, but unlike CDFGs, they are not directly executable as they only contain symbolic instructions representing application events. The Sesame environment, on the other hand, makes use of Integer-controlled Dataflow Graphs (IDF) in the mapping layer which will be discussed in great detail in Chapter 4. Another important difference between Sesame and the two mentioned environments is that the Sesame environment additionally helps the designer to prune the design space. Both the Spade and Archer environments, however lack support for this important step in architecture exploration.

2.2 Application layer

Applications in Sesame are modeled using the Kahn process network (KPN) [54] model of computation in which parallel processes – implemented in a high-level language – communicate with each other via unbounded FIFO channels. The semantics of a Kahn process network state that a process may not examine its input channel(s) for the presence of data and that it suspends its execution whenever it tries to read from an empty channel. Unlike reads, writing to channels are always successful as the channels are defined to be infinite in size. Hence at any time, a Kahn process is either *enabled*, that is executing some code or reading/writing data from/to its channels, or *blocked* waiting for data on one of its input channels. Applications built as Kahn process networks are *determinate*: the order of tokens communicated over the FIFO channels does not depend on the execution order of the processes [54]. The latter property ensures that the same input will always produce the same output irrespective of the scheduling policy employed in executing the Kahn process network. Therefore, the deterministic feature of Kahn process networks provides a lot of scheduling freedom to the designer.

Before continuing further with the discussion of Sesame's infrastructure, we first briefly review the formal representation of Kahn process networks [54], [74]. In Kahn's formalism, communication channels are represented by streams and

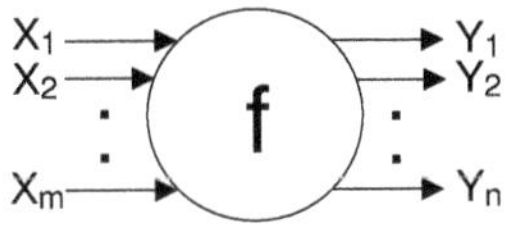

Figure 2.2: A process is a functional mapping from input streams to output streams.

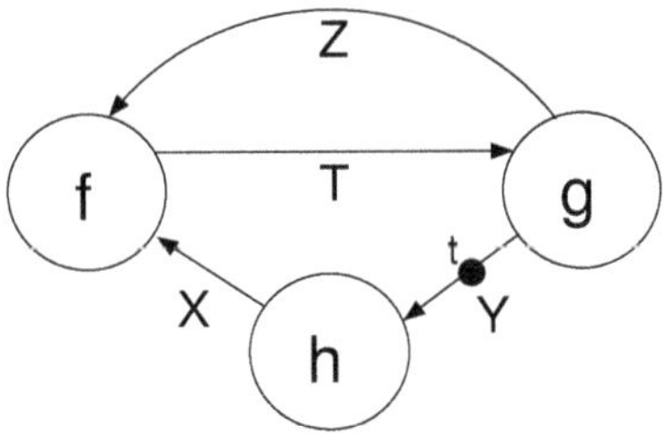

Figure 2.3: An example Kahn process network.

Kahn processes are functions which operate on streams. This formalism allows for a set of equations describing a Kahn process network. In [54], Kahn showed that the least point of these equations, which corresponds to the histories of tokens communicated over the channels, is unique. The latter means that the lengths of all streams and values of data tokens are determined only by the definition of the process network and not by the scheduling of the processes. However, the number of unconsumed tokens that can be present on communication channels does depend on the execution order.

Mathematical representation. We mainly follow the notation in [74]. A stream $X = [x_1, x_2, \ldots]$ is a sequence of data elements which can be finite or infinite in length. The symbol $\perp$ represents an empty stream. Consider a prefix ordering of sequences, where X precedes Y ($X \sqsubseteq Y$) means X is a prefix of Y. For example, $\perp \sqsubseteq [x_1] \sqsubseteq [x_1, x_2] \sqsubseteq [x_1, x_2, \ldots]$. Any increasing chain $\mathbf{X} = (X_1, X_2, \ldots)$ with $X_1 \sqsubseteq X_2 \sqsubseteq \ldots$ has a least upper bound $\sqcup\mathbf{X} = \lim_{i\to\infty} X_i$. Note that $\sqcup\mathbf{X}$ may be an infinite sequence. The set of all finite and infinite streams is a complete partial order with $\sqsubseteq$ defining the ordering. A process is a functional mapping from input streams to output streams. Figure 2.2 presents a process with m input and n output streams which can be described with the equation $(Y_1, Y_2, \ldots, Y_n) = \mathbf{f}(X_1, X_2, \ldots, X_m)$. Kahn requires that the processes be *continuous*: a process is continuous if and only if $\mathbf{f}(\sqcup\mathbf{X}) = \sqcup\mathbf{f}(\mathbf{X})$; that is, $\mathbf{f}$ maps an increasing chain into another increasing chain. Continuous functions are also *monotonic*, $X \sqsubseteq Y \Rightarrow \mathbf{f}(X) \sqsubseteq \mathbf{f}(Y)$.

Consider the Kahn process network in Figure 2.3 which can be represented by the following set of equations:

$$T = \mathbf{f}(X, Z), \tag{2.1}$$

$$(Y, Z) = \mathbf{g}(T), \tag{2.2}$$

$$X = \mathbf{h}(Y). \tag{2.3}$$

We know from [54] that if the processes are continuous mappings over a complete partial ordering, then there exists a unique least fixed point for this set of equations which corresponds to the histories of tokens produced on the communication channels. We define four continuous processes in Figure 2.4, three of which are used in Figure 2.3. It is easy to see that the equations (2.1), (2.2), and (2.3) can be combined into the following single equation

$$(Y, Z) = \mathbf{g}(\mathbf{f}(\mathbf{h}(Y), Z)), \tag{2.4}$$

which can be solved iteratively. Initial length of the stream, $(Y, Z)^0 = ([t], \perp)$, is shown in Figure 2.3.

$$(Y, Z)^1 = \mathbf{g}(\mathbf{f}(\mathbf{h}([t]), \perp)) = ([t, t], [t]), \tag{2.5}$$
$$(Y, Z)^2 = \mathbf{g}(\mathbf{f}(\mathbf{h}([t, t]), [t])) = ([t, t, t], [t, t]), \tag{2.6}$$
$$(Y, Z)^n = \mathbf{g}(\mathbf{f}(\mathbf{h}(Y^{n-1}), Z^{n-1})) = ([t, t, \ldots], [t, t, \ldots]). \tag{2.7}$$

By induction we can show that $Y = Z = [t, t, \ldots]$, and using (2.1) and (2.3) we have $Y = Z = T = X$. We find that all streams are infinite in length which consequently implies that this is a non-terminating process network. Terminating process networks have streams of finite lengths. Assume, in the previous example, that the process $\mathbf{g}$ is replaced by the process $\mathbf{g}'$ in Figure 2.4. This time a similar analysis would yield to finite streams, e.g. $(Y, Z) = ([t, t], [t])$, and the process network would terminate. This is because replacing $\mathbf{g}$ with $\mathbf{g}'$ causes a deadlock situation where all three processes block on read operations.

Because embedded systems are designed to execute over a practically infinite period of time, these applications usually involve some form of infinite loop. Hence in most cases, termination of the program indicates some kind of error for embedded applications. This is in contrast to most PC applications where the program is intended to stop after reasonable amount of run-time. Naturally, the Sesame applications, which are specified as Kahn process networks, also confirm to this non-terminating characteristic of embedded applications: one process acts as the source and provides all the input (data) to the network, and one sink process consumes all produced tokens. The successful termination of the program occurs only when the source process finishes all its input data and stops producing tokens for the network. After this incident, other processes also consume their input tokens and the program terminates. As already stated, all other program terminations point to some kind of programming and/or design errors or exceptions.

Considerable amount of research has been done in the field of application modeling, or on models of computation [64]. We have chosen for KPNs because they fit nicely to the streaming applications of the multimedia domain. Besides, KPNs are deterministic, making them independent from the scheduling (execution order) at the architecture layer. The deterministic property further guarantees the validity of event traces when the application and architecture simulators execute independently. However, KPN semantics put some restrictions on the modeling capability. They are in general not very suitable, for example, to model control dominated applications, or issues related to timing behavior such as interrupt handling cannot be captured with KPNs. KPN application models are obtained by restructuring sequential application specifications. This process of generating functionally equivalent parallel specifications (such as KPN models) from sequential code is called *code partitioning*. Code partitioning is generally a manual and time-consuming process, which often requires feedback from the application domain expert in order to identify a good partitioning.

```
Process f {
  while(1) {
    read(X,val);
    write(T,val);
    read(Z,val);
    write(T,val);
  }
}
```

```
Process h {
  while(1) {
    read(Y,val);
    write(X,val);
  }
}
```

```
Process g {
  while(1) {
    read(T,val);
    write(Z,val);
    read(T,val);
    write(Y,val);
  }
}
```

```
Process g' {
  while(1) {
    read(T,val);
    write(Y,val);
    read(T,val);
    write(Z,val);
  }
}
```

Figure 2.4: Four continuous Kahn processes. The read operator removes the first element of the stream; the write operator appends a new element at the end of the stream.

Code annotation. Because Sesame employs trace-driven co-simulation, the code of each Kahn process is equipped with annotations that describe the computational actions taken by the process. When an annotated Kahn process is executed, it records all its actions, including its communications with other Kahn processes through the FIFO channels, and consequently generates a trace of application events. This trace is a total order of events of three different types: `execute(task)`, `read(channel,data)`, and `write(channel,data)`. These manually instrumented events are the actual primitives which drive the architectural simulation. They can be used immediately to realize a high level architectural simulation, or they can be refined and the subsequent refined events may also be used. The latter usually happens, for example when we target architecture model refinement.

2.3 Architecture layer

An architecture model is constructed from generic building blocks provided by a library, which contains template performance models for processors, co-processors, memories, buffers, busses, and so on. The evaluation of an architecture is performed by simulating the performance consequences of the application events coming from the application model that is *mapped onto* the architecture model. This requires each process and channel of the Kahn process network to be associated with, or mapped onto, one component of the architecture model. When executed, each Kahn process generates a trace of events, and these event traces are routed towards a specific component of the architecture model by means of a trace event queue. A Kahn process places its application events into this queue while the corresponding architecture component consumes them. Mapping an application model onto an architecture model is illustrated in Figure 2.5. We want to emphasize once

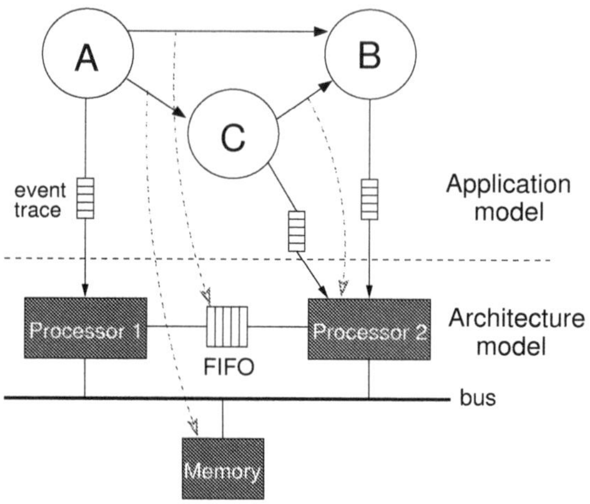

Figure 2.5: The Sesame environment: mapping an application model onto an architecture model is shown. An event-trace queue dispatches the generated application events from a Kahn process towards the architecture model component onto which it is mapped.

again that FIFO channels between the Kahn processes are also mapped (shown by the dashed arrows) in order to specify which communication medium is utilized for that data-exchange. If the source and sink processes of a FIFO channel are mapped onto the same processing component, the FIFO channel is also mapped onto the very component meaning that it is an internal communication. The latter type of communication is inexpensive as it is solely handled by the processing component and does not require access to other components in the architecture.

We stress the fact that architecture models only need to account for the timing behavior as the functional behavior is already captured by the application model which drives the co-simulation. The architecture models, implemented in our in-house simulation language Pearl [73], are highly parameterized *black box models*, which can simulate the timing characteristics of a programmable processor, a reconfigurable component, or a dedicated hardware core by simply changing the latencies associated to the incoming application events. In Figure 2.6 we show a code fragment from the implementation of a processor model in Pearl. Since Pearl is an object-based language, the code shown in Figure 2.6 embodies the class of processor objects. The processor object has two variables, `mem` and `opers` which are initialized at the creation of the object. The `mem` variable references the memory object reachable from the processor. The `opers` variable, on the other hand, refers to the list of execution times for valid operations of the processor. The processor object has three methods: `compute`, `load`, and `store`. Here the `store` method is omitted as it is similar to the `load` method. In the `compute` method, we first retrieve the execution time for the operation at hand from the `opers` variable. Then, we simulate its timing implications by the `blockt(simtime)` command. The Pearl simulation language comes with a virtual clock that keeps track of the current simulation time. When an object wants to stall for a certain time interval

```
class processor

mem :  memory
nopers :  integer   // needed for array size
opers_t = [nopers] integer   // type definition
opers :  opers_t

simtime :  integer   // local variable

compute :  (operindx:integer) -> void {
  simtime = opers[operindx];    // simulation time
  blockt(simtime);   // simulate the operation
  reply();
}

load :  (nbytes:integer,address:integer) -> void {
  mem !  load(nbytes,address);    // memory call
  reply();
}

// store method omitted

{
  while(true) {
    block(any);
  }
}
```

Figure 2.6: Pearl implementation of a generic high-level processor.

in simulated time, it calls the `blockt()` function by passing the interval as an argument. Finally, the `reply` primitive returns the control to the calling object. In the `load` method, the "`mem ! load(nbytes,address)`" statement performs a synchronous call to the memory object. Because the call is synchronous, the processor stalls until it receives a reply message from the memory. Usually the synchronous calls advance the virtual clock time, because the object called (in this case, the memory object) would account for the time it takes to perform the requested operation before replying back to the calling object. Further information on the Pearl language is presented in Section 2.5 within the scope of the architecture simulator.

The architecture components in Sesame typically operate at the bus-arbitration level which is defined within transaction level modeling (TLM) [17]. This means that the simulation times associated to computation and communication events coming from the application model are approximate, that is in most cases not cycle-accurate. As shown, the architecture models are quite generic; thus by just changing latencies assigned to incoming application events, a template processor model can well be used to simulate the timing behavior of a programmable processor, reconfigurable implementation, or dedicated hardware execution at the bus-arbitration level. This allows a designer to quickly evaluate different hardware/software partitionings at a high level of abstraction by just altering the latencies assigned to

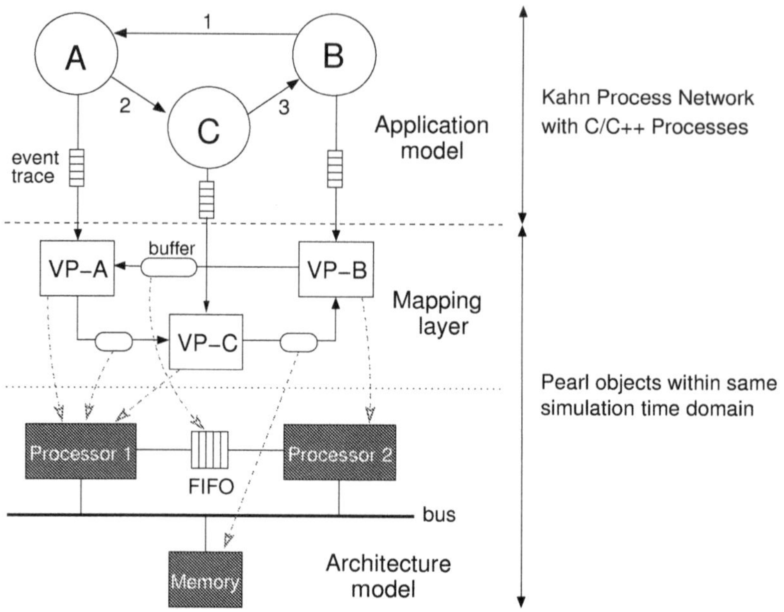

Figure 2.7: Sesame's application model layer, architecture model layer, and the mapping layer which is an interface between application and architecture models.

application events. These latencies can be obtained from a lower level model of an architecture component, from performance estimation tools, from available documentation, or from an experienced designer. In Section 2.7 we propose and argue an approach, where we obtain latency numbers for a certain programmable core by coupling Sesame with a *low-level* instruction-level simulator.

Sesame further supports gradual architecture model refinement. As a designer takes decisions towards his final design, decisions such as which parts to be realized in hardware and which parts in software, some components of the architecture model may be refined. This means that the architecture model starts to reflect the characteristics of a particular implementation. While some of the components at the black box level are refined in order to reflect the decisions taken and the level of detail needed, the application events driving these components should also be refined. Sesame has some support for such event refinement and we postpone further discussion on this until Chapter 4 which is entirely dedicated to this issue. However, we should point out that gradual model refinement is an active research field and is still in its early stages.

2.4 Mapping layer

In Sesame there is an additional layer between the application model and architecture model layers, acting as a supporting interface in the process of mapping Kahn processes, i.e. their event traces, onto architecture model components. This intermediate layer also takes care of the run-time scheduling of application events when multiple Kahn processes are mapped onto a single architecture component. This intermediate layer is called the *mapping layer* and it comprises of virtual processors (abbreviated as VP in Figure 2.7) and FIFO buffers for communication between the virtual processors. As illustrated in Figure 2.7, there is a one-to-one relationship between the Kahn processes in the application model and the virtual processors in the mapping layer. The same is true for the Kahn channels and the FIFO buffers in the mapping layer. However, the size of the FIFO buffers in the mapping layer is parameterized and dependent on the architecture, while the size of the Kahn channels is by definition infinite and independent of the architecture. In practice, the size of the FIFO buffers are set to sufficiently large values so that whenever a virtual processor issues a write operation, there is always room available in the target buffer and the write operation succeeds immediately. One can try to accomplish this by gradually increasing the size of all FIFO buffers until there occurs no blocking write operation. However, it may, in general, be practically impossible to decide on the buffer sizes at design time. Then, runtime mechanisms for handling these so called "artificial deadlocks" are needed. Most of the proposed runtime mechanisms [43], [74] try to find a chain of causes, that is the processes involved in a mutual "wait for" situation, in order to resolve the deadlock.

The events dispatched by a Kahn process are read from the trace event queue by the corresponding virtual processor at the mapping layer. It is the virtual processor which forwards the application events and hence drives the architecture model component for co-simulation. This mechanism ensures deadlock free scheduling when application events from different event traces are merged. In order to see how deadlocks may occur, consider the following scenario with the three Kahn processes in Figure 2.7. In this scenario, Processes A and C are mapped onto Processor 1, Process B is mapped onto Processor 2, and first come first serve (FCFS) event scheduling policy is employed at the architecture layer. Assume that the following events take place in chronological order:

- Process A dispatches R_1, that represents reading data from channel 1,
- Process C dispatches W_3, writing data to channel 3,
- Process B dispatches two consecutive events, first R_3 followed by a W_1.

If there are no initial tokens on the channels 1 and 3, this would yield a deadlock situation as both processors would be waiting for data from each other. This is because, the blocking read semantics of the Kahn process networks are also reflected at the architecture layer. In order to avoid such deadlocks, a virtual processor does not immediately dispatch communication events. It first checks the corresponding buffer in the mapping layer to determine if the communication is safe or not. For a communication to be safe, there should be data available for read events and, similarly, there must be room available for write events in the target buffer. If the communication is not safe, the virtual processor blocks. This is possible because, as shown in Figure 2.7, both the mapping layer and the architecture layer are implemented in Pearl and share the same simulation time domain. The computation events however are always immediately dispatched to the architecture model as they do not cause any deadlocks. Each time a virtual processor dispatches an application event (either computation or communication) to an architecture model component, it is blocked in simulation time until the event's latency is simulated by the architecture model. This introduces a tightly coupled relation between the virtual processor and the related architecture model component. As a consequence, architecture model components account only for computational and pure communication latencies (e.g. bus arbitration and data transfer latencies), while latencies due to synchronization are captured at the mapping layer. Currently, for scheduling events from different Kahn processes, processing components in the architecture model employ FCFS policy by default. However, any other preferred scheduling policy can also be used.

Previously, we have mentioned that Sesame supports gradual architecture model refinement. As we will show in Chapter 4, this is achieved by refining the virtual processors at the mapping layer. This allows us to include more implementation details in order to perform simulations at multiple levels of abstraction. With respect to refinement in Sesame, the basic idea is to open up a virtual processor and to incorporate a dataflow graph which is capable of i) transferring more application-level information to the architecture level ii) and also exploiting this information to perform architectural simulations at different levels of abstraction. Because this approach is flexible in the sense that only virtual processors of interest are refined, it naturally allows for mixed-level simulations, where one or more architecture component(s) operate(s) at a different level of abstraction than the rest of the model components. As a consequence, mixed-level simulations avoid building a complete, detailed architecture model during the early design stages, and foster system-evaluation efficiency by only refining the necessary parts of the architecture.

2.5 Implementation aspects

In the previous sections we have seen that Sesame is composed of three layers: application model layer, architecture model layer, and the mapping layer which is an interface between the two previous layers. All three layers in Sesame are composed of components which should be instantiated and connected using some form of object creation and initialization mechanism. Because the Y-chart methodology requires the system designer to rapidly build and evaluate system-level simulation models, Sesame facilitates such easy construction by making use of libraries (e.g. a library of architecture model components may include pre-built Pearl code for processors, different types of memories, interconnection components at various levels of abstraction, or a library of application model components may include common processes from the media application domain such as pre-built processes for discrete cosine and fourier transforms) and a flexible description format for connecting these components.

The structure of Sesame's simulation models[1] is defined in YML (Y-chart Modeling Language) [23] which is an XML based language. Using XML is attractive

[1] We use the term simulation model as a generic term to refer to both application and architecture models in Sesame.

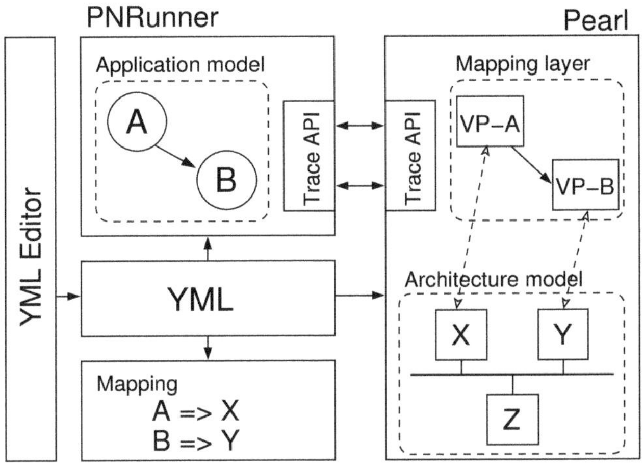

Figure 2.8: Sesame software overview. Sesame's model description language YML is used to describe the application model, the architecture model, and the mapping which relates the two models for co-simulation.

because it is simple and flexible, reinforces reuse of model descriptions, and comes with good programming language support. An overview of the Sesame software framework is given in Figure 2.8, where we use YML to describe the application model, the architecture model, and the mapping which relates the two models for co-simulation. YML describes simulation models as directed graphs. The core elements of YML are `network`, `node`, `port`, `link`, and `property`. YML files containing only these elements are called flat YML. There are two additional elements `set` and `script` which were added to equip YML with scripting support to simplify the description of complicated models, e.g. a complex interconnect with a large number of nodes. We now briefly describe these YML elements.

- `network`: Network elements contain graphs of nodes and links, and may also contain subnetworks which create hierarchy in the model description. A network element requires a `name` and optionally a `class` attribute. Names must be unique in a network for they are used as identifiers.

- `node`: Node elements represent building blocks (or components) of a simulation model. Kahn processes in an application model or components in an architecture model are represented by nodes in their respective YML description files. Node elements also require a `name` and usually a `class` attribute which are used by the simulators to identify the node type. For example, in Figure 2.9, the class attribute of node A specifies that it is a C++ (application) process.

- `port`: Port elements add connection points to nodes and networks. They require `name` and `dir` attributes. The `dir` attribute defines the direction of the port and may have values *in* or *out*. Port names must also be unique in a node or network.

- `link`: Link elements connect ports. They require `innode`, `inport`, `outnode`, and `outport` attributes. The `innode` and `outnode` attributes denote the names of nodes (or subnetworks) to be connected. Ports used for the connection are specified by `inport` and `outport`.

- `property`: Property elements provide additional information for YML objects. Certain simulators may require certain information on parameter values. For example, Sesame's architecture simulator needs to read an array of execution latencies for each processor component in order to associate timing values to incoming application events. In Figure 2.9, the *ProcessNetwork* element has a *library* property which specifies the name of the shared library where the object code belonging to *ProcessNetwork*, e.g. object codes of its node elements *A*, *B*, and *C* reside. Property elements require `name` and `value` attributes.

- `script`: The script element supports Perl as a scripting language for YML. The text encapsulated by the script element is processed by the Perl interpreter in the order it appears in the YML file. The script element has no attributes. The namings in `name`, `class`, and `value` attributes that begin with a '$' are evaluated as global Perl variables within the current context of the Perl interpreter. Therefore, users should take good care to avoid name conflicts. The script element is usually used together with the following set element in order to create complex network structures. Figure 2.10 gives such an example, which will be explained below.

- `set`: The set element provides a for-loop like structure to define YML structures which simplifies complex network descriptions. It requires three attributes `init`, `cond`, and `loop`. YML interprets the values of these attributes as a script element. The `init` is evaluated once at the beginning of set element processing, `cond` is evaluated at the beginning of every iteration and is considered as a boolean. The processing of a set element stops when its `cond` is false or 0. The `loop` attribute is evaluated at the end of each iteration.

The YML description of the process network in Figure 2.8 is shown in Figure 2.9. The process network defined has three C++ processes, each associated with input and output ports, which are connected through the link elements and embedded in *ProcessNetwork*. Figure 2.10 illustrates the usage of `set` and `script` for Sesame's architecture simulator, creating ten processors each with one input and output port when embedded in the architecture description YML. Both of Sesame's (application and architecture) simulators can make use of `set` and `script` elements. Hence, one could as well use these elements to create complex process networks. What is more, using `set` and `script` parameterized component network descriptions can be realized. This is achieved by parameterizing the loop sizes which can be supplied by the user at run time. For example, one can define an NxM crossbar and reuse it in different simulations by initializing it with different N and M values, which would further foster reuse of model descriptions.

```
<network name="ProcessNetwork" class="KPN">
  <property name="library" value="libPN.so"/>

  <node name="A" class="CPP_Process">
    <port name="port0" dir="in"/>
    <port name="port1" dir="out"/>
  </node>
  <node name="B" class="CPP_Process">
    <port name="port0" dir="in"/>
    <port name="port1" dir="out"/>
  </node>
  <node name="C" class="CPP_Process">
    <port name="port0" dir="in"/>
    <port name="port1" dir="out"/>
  </node>

  <link innode="B" inport="port1"
      outnode="A" outport="port0"/>
  <link innode="A" inport="port1"
      outnode="C" outport="port0"/>
  <link innode="C" inport="port1"
      outnode="B" outport="port0"/>
</network>
```

Figure 2.9: YML description of process network in Figure 2.7.

In addition to structural descriptions, YML is also used to specify mapping descriptions, that is relating application tasks to architecture model components.

- `mapping`: Mapping elements identify application and architecture simulators. They require `side` and `name` attributes to be specified. The `side` attribute can have a value of either *source* or *dest*, while the `name` attribute is a string specifying the name of the corresponding simulator. In Figure 2.11, we give the YML mapping specification for the simple example in Figure 2.8, where two application processes are mapped onto two architecture model components connected by a bus. In this mapping specification, the application (architecture) side is defined as *source* (*dest*), whereas the opposite matching was also possible.

- `map`: Map elements map application nodes (model components) onto archi-

```
<set init="$i = 0" cond="$i &lt; 10" loop="$i++">
  <script>
    $nodename="processor$i"
  <script/>
  <node name="$nodename" class="pearl_object">
    <port name="port0" dir="in"/>
    <port name="port1" dir="out"/>
  </node>
</set>
```

Figure 2.10: An example illustrating the usage of set and script elements.

```
<mapping side="source" name="application">
  <mapping side="dest" name="architecture">
    <map source="A" dest="X">
      <port source="portA" dest="portBus"/>
    </map>
    <map source="B" dest="Y">
      <port source="portB" dest="portBus"/>
    </map>
    <instruction source="op_A" dest="op_A"/>
    <instruction source="op_B" dest="op_B"/>
  </mapping>
</mapping>
```

Figure 2.11: The mapping YML which realizes the mapping in Figure 2.8.

tecture nodes. They require `source` and `dest` attributes which specify the name of the components in the corresponding simulators. The node mapping in Figure 2.8, that is mapping processes A and B onto processors X and Y, is given in Figure 2.11 where `source` (`dest`) refers to the application (architecture) side.

- `port`: Port elements relate application ports to architecture ports. When an application node is mapped onto an architecture node, the connection points (or ports) also need to be mapped in order to specify which communication medium should be used in the architecture model simulator. To realize this mapping, as shown in Figure 2.8, port elements require `source` and `dest` attributes.

- `instruction`: Instruction elements require `source` and `dest` attributes and are used to specify computation and communication events generated by the application simulator and consumed by the architecture simulator. As already discussed in Section 2.1, these events represent the workload imposed by the application onto the evaluated architecture. Hence, this element maps application event names onto architecture event names.

2.5.1 Application simulator

Sesame's application simulator is called *PNRunner*, or process network runner. PNRunner implements the semantics of Kahn process networks in C++. It reads a YML application description file and executes the application model described there. The object code of each process is fetched from a shared library whose name is also specified in the YML description file. For example, for the process network in Figure 2.9, the associated shared library is specified as "libPN.so" in the given YML description. PNRunner currently supports only C++ processes. However, to implement the processes, any language for which a process loader class is written can be used. This is because PNRunner relies on the loader classes for process executions. Besides, from the perspective of PNRunner, data communicated through the channels is typed as "blocks of bytes". Interpretation of data

```
class Idct:  public Process {
  InPort<Block> blockInP;
  OutPort<Block> blockOutP;
  // private member function
  void idct (short* block);

  public:
    Idct(const class Id& n, In<Block>& blockinF,
      Out<Block>& blockOutF);
    const char* type() const {return "Idct";}
    void main();
};

// constructor
Idct::Idct(const class Id& n, In<Block>& blockInF,
  Out<Block>& blockOutF)
    :  Process(n), blockInP(id("blockInP"), blockInF),
      blockOutP(id("blockOutP"), blockOutF)
{ }

// main member function
void Idct::main() {
  Block tmpblock;

  while(true) {
    read(blockInP,tmpblock);
    idct(tmpblock.data);
    execute("IDCT");
    write(blockOutP,tmpblock);
  }
}
```

Figure 2.12: C++ code for the IDCT process taken from an H.263 decoder process network application. The process reads block of data from its input port, performs an IDCT operation on the data, and writes transformed data to its output port.

types is done by processes and process loaders. As already shown in Figure 2.9, the class attribute of a node informs PNRunner which process loader it should use. In this example, all three processes are implemented in C++. Currently, the implemented C++ process loader supports part of the YAPI interface [27], which is an API (provided with a runtime support system) developed at Philips Research for writing Kahn process network applications. YAPI specifies process network structures implicitly in C++ source code, and differs from PNRunner mainly in this perspective. Because restructuring C++ code is, in most cases, more time consuming than rewriting YML descriptions, YAPI's method is less flexible in terms of model reuse. As PNRunner supports the more favorable YML, it does not support YAPI's implicit process network description. Similar to YAPI, PNRunner provides threading support and interprocess communication (IPC) primitives and supports most of the remaining parts of YAPI. Due to this high degree of YAPI support, YAPI applications are easily converted to PNRunner applications.

Sesame's C++ process loader is aware of the necessary YML specifications.

From the YML application description, it uses the *library* property which specifies the shared library containing the process codes, and the `name` attributes for nodes that point to the class names which implement the processes. In order to pass arguments to the process constructors (part of YAPI support) or to the processes themselves, the property *arg* has been added to YML. Process classes are loaded through generated stub code. In Figure 2.12 we present the IDCT process from an H.263 decoder application. It is derived from the parent class *Process* which provides a common interface. Following YAPI, ports are template classes to set the type of data exchanged. If two communicating ports have different data types, this generates an error message.

As can be seen in Figure 2.8, PNRunner also provides a trace API to drive an architecture simulator. Using this API, PNRunner can send application events to the architecture simulator where their performance consequences are simulated. Hence, application/architecture co-simulation is possible, but one could also first run the application simulator, store the generated event traces, and subsequently run the architecture simulator. However, this approach requires one to store event traces which can be cumbersome for long simulations. While reading data from or writing data to ports, PNRunner also generates a communication event as a side effect. Hence, communication events are automatically generated. However, computation events must be signaled explicitly by the processes. This can be achieved by annotating the process code with *execute(char *)* statements. In the main function of the IDCT process in Figure 2.12, we show a typical example. This process first reads a block of data from port *blockInP*, performs an IDCT operation on the data, and writes output data to port *blockOutP*. The *read* and *write* functions, as a side effect, automatically generate the communication events. However, we have added the function call *execute("IDCT")* to record that an IDCT operation is performed. The string passed to the *execute* function represents the type of the execution event and needs to match to the operations defined in the application YML file.

2.5.2 Architecture simulator

In Section 2.3 we have seen that architecture models in Sesame are implemented in the Pearl discrete event simulation language [23]. Pearl is a small but powerful object-based language which provides easy construction of abstract architecture models and fast performance simulation. It has a C-like syntax with a few additional primitives for simulation purposes. A Pearl program is a collection of concurrent objects which communicate with each other through message-passing. Pearl objects execute sequential code that is specified in class specifications. Each object has its own data space which cannot be directly accessed by other objects. The objects send messages to other objects to communicate, e.g. to request some data or operation. The called object may then perform the request, and if expected, may also reply to the calling object.

Communication between objects is performed by synchronous or asynchronous messages. After sending an asynchronous message, the sending object continues execution, while in synchronous communication it waits for a reply message from the receiver. An asynchronous message is of the form:

```
dest !!  amethod(par1,...,parn);
```

This statement sends an asynchronous message to an object called `dest` by calling its method `amethod` with the parameters $\texttt{par}_1$, ..., $\texttt{par}_n$. Naturally, the method `amethod` is defined in the class specification of the object `dest`. Pearl objects have message queues where all received messages are collected. By explicitly executing a `block` statement, a Pearl object may wait for messages to arrive. Hence, a receiving object itself decides if and when it performs the "remote method call" by other objects. For example,

```
block(method1,method2);
```

causes the object to block until a message calling either `method1` or `method2` arrives. To refer all methods of an object, the keyword `any` can be used in a `block` statement. In the case of multiple messages in the message queue, Pearl handles messages by default with FCFS policy. Adapting other policies is possible but not straightforward. To do this, objects should first store the incoming messages using an internal data structure, and then do the reordering themselves before handling them.

Similarly, an object sends a synchronous message using

```
r = dest !  amethod(par1,...,parn);
```

after which it blocks until the receiver replies to this message using the statement

```
reply(r_value);
```

The sender then continues execution with the next statement after the synchronous call.

To support discrete-event simulations, the Pearl runtime system maintains a virtual clock which keeps track of the current simulation time. In accordance with the discrete-event model, the simulation clock advances in discrete steps and never goes backwards in time. Pearl objects signal to the runtime system that they want to wait an interval in simulation time and that they do not want to be rescheduled during that period by calling a `blockt` statement. Hence, an object that wants to wait 10 time units executes

```
blockt(10);
```

When all objects are waiting for the clock (`blockt` statement) or messages (`block` statement), the runtime system advances the clock to the first time that some object will become active. When all objects wait for messages, meaning that none of the objects can become active in the future due to deadlock, the simulation is terminated.

At the end of simulation, the Pearl runtime system outputs a postmortem analysis of the simulation results. For this purpose, it keeps track of some statistical information such as utilization of objects (idle/busy times), contention (busy objects with pending messages), profiling (time spent in object methods), critical path analysis, and average bandwidth between objects.

If we compare Pearl's programming paradigm and associated primitives to those of the popular SystemC v2.0 language, we observe that Pearl follows a higher level of abstraction for certain tasks. First, by implementing the aforementioned *remote method calling* through the message-passing mechanism, Pearl abstracts away the concept of ports and explicit channels connecting ports as employed in SystemC. Second, the remote method calling technique of Pearl leads to autonomous objects in terms of execution, i.e. the object determines itself if and when it should process an incoming message. Third, buffering of messages in the object message queues is handled implicitly by the Pearl run-time system, whereas in SystemC one has to implement explicit buffering. Finally, Pearl's message passing primitives lucidly incorporate inter-object synchronization, while separate event notifications are needed in SystemC. As a consequence of these abstractions, Pearl is, with respect to SystemC, less prone to programming errors. In order to take advantage of this, the SCPEx (SystemC Pearl Extension) language [97] has recently been built on top of SystemC v2.0, which equips SystemC models with Pearl primitives and its message-passing paradigm.

2.6 Mapping decision support

System-level simulation, no matter how effective and rapid evaluation technique it actually is, will inevitably fail to explore large parts of the design space. This is because each system simulation only evaluates a single decision point in the maximal design space of the early stages. Because it is infeasible to simulate every candidate in most practical cases, it is extremely important that some direction is provided to the designer which will guide him towards potentially promising solutions. Analytical methods may be of great help here, as they can be utilized to identify a small set of promising candidates. The designer then only needs to focus on this small set, for which he can construct simulation models at multiple levels of abstraction. Subsequently, through gradual model refinements he can achieve the desired level of accuracy (in his evaluations), perform iterative simulations for reciprocal comparison of the candidate points, and finally (and optimistically) reach the most favorable solution. The process of trimming down an exponential design space to some finite set is called *design space pruning*, and has recently been a hot research topic [44], [2], [37].

In Sesame effective steering is most needed during the mapping decision stage. In this stage a designer needs to make the most critical decisions: selection of the platform architecture and the mapping of the application onto the selected architecture. Without using any analytical method it is very hard to make these decisions which will seriously affect the design process, and in turn the success of the final design. Moreover, coping with the tight constraints of embedded systems, there exist multiple criteria to consider, like the processing time, power consumption, and cost of the architecture, all of which further complicate the mapping decision. In Chapter 3, we develop a mathematical model to capture the trade-offs during the mapping stage in Sesame. In our model, these trade-offs, namely the maximum processing time, power consumption, and cost of the architecture are formulated as the multiple conflicting objectives of the mapping decision problem. With the help of experiments with two multimedia applications, we will show the effectiveness and usefulness of design space pruning by analytical modeling and multiobjective optimization.

2.7 Obtaining numbers for system-level simulation

We know from Section 2.3 that an architecture model in Sesame only needs to account for the timing behavior since it is driven by an application model which captures the functional behavior. An architecture model component actually assigns latency values to the incoming application events that comprise the computation and communication operations to be simulated. This is accomplished by parameterizing each architecture model component with a table of operation latencies. In this table there is an entry for each possible operation, such as the latency of performing an IDCT operation (computation), or the latency of accessing a memory element (communication). By simply changing these latencies (i.e. using lower latencies for hardware and higher latencies for software implementations) one can experiment with different hardware/software partitionings at the system-level. Therefore, regarding the accuracy of system-level performance evaluation it is important that these latencies correctly reflect the speed of their corresponding architecture components. We now briefly discuss two possible techniques (one for software and another one for hardware implementations) which can be deployed to attain latencies with good accuracy.

The first technique that we discuss here can be used to calibrate the latencies of programmable components in the architecture model, such as microprocessors, DSPs, application specific instruction processors (ASIPs) and so on. The calibration idea is quite simple and straightforward as depicted in Figure 2.13(a). It requires that the designer has access to the C/C++ cross compiler and low level (ISS/RTL) simulator of the target processor. In the figure we have chosen to calibrate the latency value(s) of (Kahn) process C which is mapped to some kind of processor for which we have a cross compiler and an ISS simulator. First, we take the source code of process C, add basically two statements (*send-data* and *receive-data*) for UNIX IPC-based communication (that is to realize the interprocess communication between the two simulators: PNRunner and the ISS simulator), and generate binary code using the cross compiler. The code of process C in PNRunner is also modified (now called process C''). Process C'' now simply forwards its input data to the ISS simulator, blocks until it receives processed data from the ISS simulator, and then writes received data to its output Kahn channels. Hence, process C'' leaves all computations to the ISS simulator, which additionally records the number of cycles taken for the computations while performing them. Because two distinct simulators from different abstraction levels are simultaneously used to simulate a single application, the resulting means of operation is called a *mixed-level simulation*. Once the mixed-level simulation is finished, recordings of the ISS simulator can be analyzed statistically, e.g. the arithmetic means of the measured code fragments can be taken as the latency for the corresponding architecture com-

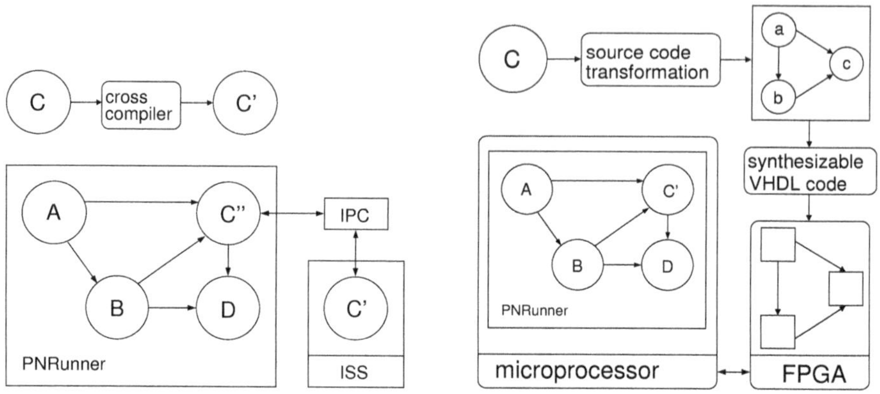

(a) Solution for software implementations.

(b) Solution for hardware implementations.

Figure 2.13: Obtaining low level numbers.

ponent in the system-level architecture model. This scheme can be easily extended to an application/architecture mixed-level co-simulation using a recently proposed technique called *trace calibration* [98].

The second calibration technique makes use of reconfigurable computing with field programmable gate arrays or FPGAs. Reconfigurable computing is based on the idea that some part of hardware can be configured at run time to efficiently perform a task at hand. When the current task is finished, the hardware can be *reconfigured* to perform another task. Due to this high flexibility, FPGAs are commonly used in early stages of hardware design, such as application specific integrated circuit (ASIC) prototyping. Figure 2.13(b) illustrates the calibration technique for hardware components. This time it is assumed that the process C is to be implemented in hardware. First, the application programmer takes the source code of process C and performs source code transformations on it, which unveils the inherent task-level parallelism within the process C. These transformations, starting from a single process, create a functionally equivalent (Kahn) process network with processes at finer granularities. The abstraction level of the processes is lowered such that a one-to-one mapping of the process network to an FPGA platform becomes possible. There are already some prototype environments which can accomplish these steps for certain applications. For example, the Compaan tool [57], [90] can automatically perform process network transformations while the Laura [106] and ESPAM [ref] tools can generate VHDL code from a process network specification. This VHDL code can then be synthesized and mapped onto an FPGA using commercial synthesis tools. Mapping process C onto an FPGA and executing the remaining processes of the original process network on a microprocessor (e.g., FPGA board connected to a computer using PCI bus, or processor core embedded into the FPGA), statistics on the hardware implementation of process C can be collected.

Actually, we report experimental results in Chapter 5, where we use this technique in order to calibrate and verify some of our system-level simulation models.

2.8 Summary

In this chapter we provided an overview of our modeling and simulation environment – Sesame. Within the context of Sesame, we discussed the increasingly popular Y-chart modeling methodology and introduced key concepts such as design space pruning, gradual model refinement, trace-driven co-simulation, and so on. We then proceeded with discussing the three-layer architecture of Sesame in detail, together with some useful background information when needed (e.g. intermezzo on Kahn process networks). This discussion was followed by the discussion on the implementation aspects, i.e. the software architecture of Sesame: application and architecture simulators, and the usage of XML for simulation model descriptions and mapping specifications. A few keywords from this part of the discussion are the Process Network Runner (PNRunner), Pearl discrete-event simulation language, and the Y-chart Modeling Language (YML). In the coming chapters our focus will be on the research carried out both using Sesame and also within Sesame.

3

Multiobjective application mapping

In this chapter we focus on *design space pruning*, that is, in most general terms, to trim down an exponential design space into a finite set of points, which are more interesting (or superior) with respect to some chosen design criteria. Because Sesame maintains independent application and architecture models and relies on the co-simulation of these two models in the performance evaluation of the composed embedded system, it is in need of an explicit mapping step which relates each Kahn process and channel in the application model to a processor/memory component in the architecture model. Each mapping decision taken in this step corresponds to a single point in the design space. In order to achieve an optimal design, the designer should ideally evaluate and compare every single point in this space. However, this exhaustive search quickly becomes infeasible, as the design space grows exponentially with the sizes of both application and architecture model components.

Until recently the Sesame environment has relied on the traditional design approach which states that the mapping step is to be performed by an experienced designer, intuitively. However, this assumption was increasingly becoming inappropriate for efficient design space exploration. First of all, the Sesame environment targets exploration at an early design stage where the design space is very large. At this stage, it is very hard to make critical decisions such as *mapping* without using any analytical method or a design tool, since these decisions seriously affect the rest of the design process, and in turn, the success of the final design. Besides, modern embedded systems are already quite complicated, generally having a heterogeneous combination of hardware and software parts possibly with dynamic behavior. It is also very likely that these embedded systems will become even more complex in the (near) future, and intuitive mapping decisions will eventually become unfeasible for future designs. Moreover, coping with the design constraints of embedded systems, there exist multiple criteria to consider, like the processing times, power consumption and cost of the architecture, all of which further complicate the mapping decision.

In Sesame, these issues are captured by means of a multiobjective combinatorial optimization problem [35]. Due to its large size and nonlinear nature, it is realized that the integration of a fast and accurate optimizer is of crucial importance for this problem. The primary aim of the multiobjective optimization process is to provide the designer with a set of tradable solutions, rather than a single optimal point. Evolutionary algorithms (EAs) seem to be a good choice for attacking such problems, as they evolve over a population rather than a single solution. For this reason, numerous multiobjective evolutionary algorithms (MOEAs) [22] have been proposed in the literature. The earlier MOEAs such as VEGA [85], MOGA [41], and NSGA [88] have been followed by the elitist versions, e.g., NSGA-II [29] and SPEA2 [109]. More recent work has focused on the possible performance improvements by incorporating sophisticated strategies into MOEAs. For example, Jensen has employed advanced data structures to improve the run-time complexity of some popular MOEAs (e.g. NSGA-II) [53], while Yen et al. have proposed an approach based on the usage of dynamic populations [104]. In another recent work [69], the idea of transforming a high-dimensional multiobjective problem into a biobjective optimization problem is exploited within an MOEA.

This chapter is mainly based on [35], [37] and has the following contributions:

- First, a mathematical model is developed to formulate the multiprocessor mapping problem under multiple objectives.

- We employ two state-of-the-art MOEAs [29], [109] in two case studies from system-on-chip (SoC) design, and report performance results. Previously, these MOEAs have mostly been tested on simple and well-known mathematical functions, but detailed performance results on real life engineering problems from different domains are very rare if any.

- In order to determine the accuracy of the MOEAs, the mathematical model is first linearized and then solved by using an exact method, namely the lexicographic weighted Tchebycheff method.

- We perform two case studies in which we demonstrate i) the successful application of MOEAs to SoC design, especially in the early stages where the design space is very large, ii) the quantitative performance analysis of two state-of-the-art MOEAs examined in conjunction with an exact approach with respect to multiple criteria (e.g., accuracy, coverage of design space), and iii) the verification of multiobjective optimization results by further investigating a number of tradable solutions by means of simulation.

- In addition, we perform comparative experiments on variation operators and report performance results for different crossover types and mutation usage. More specifically, we analyze the consequences of using one-point, two-point and uniform crossover operators on MOEA convergence and exploration of the search space. Besides, we also show that mutation still remains as a vital operator in multiobjective search to achieve good exploration. Hence, the MOEAs stay in accordance with the standard EAs in this respect.

- We define three new metrics which will allow us to compare different aspects of MOEAs.
- We examine the performance consequences of using different fitness assignment schemes (finer-grained and computationally more expensive vs. more coarse-grained and computationally less expensive) in MOEAs.
- We study the outcome of using three different repair algorithms in constraint handling and compare them with respect to multiple criteria such as convergence and coverage of search space.

The rest of this chapter is organized as follows. Section 3.1 discusses related work. Problem and model definitions and constraint linearizations are described in Section 3.2. Section 3.3 consists of four parts discussing the preliminaries for multiobjective optimization, the lexicographic weighted Tchebycheff method, the different attributes of multiobjective evolutionary algorithms and the repair algorithm, and the metrics for comparing nondominated sets. In Section 3.4, two case studies are performed, comparative performance analysis of MOEAs are given, followed by some simulation results. The last section presents concluding remarks.

3.1 Related work on pruning and exploration

In the domain of embedded systems and hardware/software co-design, several studies have been performed for *system-level synthesis* [13], [30], [96] and *platform configuration* [45], [44], [2], [95]. The former means the problem of optimally mapping a task-level specification onto a heterogeneous hardware/software architecture, while the latter includes tuning the platform architecture parameters and exploring its configuration space.

Blickle et al. [13] partition the synthesis problem into two steps: the selection of the architecture (allocation), and the mapping of the algorithm onto the selected architecture in space (binding) and time (scheduling). In their framework, they only consider cost and speed of the architecture, power consumption is ignored. To cope with infeasibility, they use penalty functions which reduce the number of infeasible individuals to an acceptable degree. In [96], a similar synthesis approach is applied to evaluate the design tradeoffs in packet processor architectures. But additionally, this model includes a real-time calculus to reason about packet streams and their processing.

In the MOGAC framework [30], starting from a task graph specification, the synthesis problem is solved for three objectives: cost, speed and power consumption of the target architecture. To accomplish this, an adaptive genetic algorithm which can escape local minima is utilized. However, this framework lacks the management of possible infeasibility as it treats all non-dominated solutions equally even if they violate hard constraints. No repair algorithm is used in any stage of the search process, the invalid individuals are just removed at the end of evolution.

In [45], the configuration space of a parameterized system-on-chip (SoC) architecture is optimized with respect to a certain application mapped onto that architecture. The exploration takes into account power/performance trade-offs and takes advantage of parameter dependencies to guide the search. The configuration space is first clustered by means of a dependency graph, and each cluster is searched exhaustively for local Pareto-optimal solutions. In the second step, the clusters are merged iteratively until a single cluster remains. The Pareto-optimal configurations within this last cluster form the global Pareto-optimal solutions. In [44], the exploration framework of [45] is used in combination with a simulation framework. The simulation models of SoC components (e.g. processors, memories, interconnect busses) are used to capture dynamic information which is essential for the computation of power and performance metrics. More recently, Ascia et al. [2] have also applied a genetic algorithm to solve the same problem.

The work in [95] presents an exploration algorithm for parameterized memory architectures. The inputs to the exploration algorithm are timing and energy constraints obtained from the application tasks and the memory architecture specifications. The goal is to identify the system time/energy trade-off, when each task data member is assigned a target memory component. Exact and heuristic algorithms are given for solving different instances of the problem. However, only one type of heuristic (based on a branch and bound algorithm) is used, and no comparison with other heuristics is given.

In the Sesame framework, we do not target the problem of system synthesis. Therefore, a schedule is not constructed at the end of the design process. Our aim is to develop a methodology which allows for evaluating a large design space and provides us with a number of approximated Pareto-optimal solutions. These solutions are then input to our simulation framework for further evaluation. After simulation, figures about system-level trade-offs (e.g. utilization of components, data throughput, communication media contention) are provided to the designer. Thus, our goal is efficient system-level performance evaluation by means of design space pruning and exploration. In addition, our framework also differs from the mentioned frameworks in the sense that it uses process networks for algorithm specification rather than task graphs.

Most of the aforementioned system-level synthesis/exploration and platform configuration frameworks have relied on evolutionary search techniques. Besides these studies, evolutionary algorithms are utilized at many abstraction levels of electronic systems design, such as in analog integrated circuit synthesis [1] and in the design of digital signal processing (DSP) systems [14] and evolvable hardware [42].

3.2 Problem and model definition

From Chapter 2, we know that an embedded system, which is under evaluation in Sesame, is defined in terms of an application model describing the system's *functional behavior* (what the system is supposed to do), and an architecture model which defines system's hardware resources (how it does it) and captures its *timing characteristics*. Because of this clear-cut utilization of application and architecture models, Sesame needs an explicit mapping step to relate these models for co-simulation. In this step, the designer decides for each application process and FIFO channel a destination architecture model component to simulate its workload. Thus, this step is one of the most important stages in the design process, since the final success of the design is highly dependent on these mapping choices. In Figure 3.1, we illustrate this mapping step on a very simple example. In this example, the application model consists of four Kahn processes and five FIFO channels. The architecture model contains two processors and one shared memory. To decide on an optimum mapping, there exist multiple criteria to consider: maximum processing time in the system, power consumption and the total cost of the architecture. This section aims at defining a mapping function, shown with **f** in Figure 3.1, to supply the designer with a set of best alternative mappings under the mentioned system criteria. It is clear from Figure 3.1, even without taking into account any system criteria, that the number of alternative mappings, i.e. the size of the design space, is extremely large as it grows exponentially with the sizes of the application and architecture model components. Hence, mapping a moderate size application with a few tens of nodes and channels onto a platform architecture with a few processing cores immediately yields an intractable design space, which in turn eliminates the alternative exhaustive search option.

3.2.1 Application modeling

The application models in Sesame are represented by a graph $KPN = (V_K, E_K)$ where the set V_K and E_K refer to the Kahn nodes and the directed FIFO channels between these nodes, respectively. For each node $a \in V_K$, we define $B_a \subseteq E_K$ to be the set of FIFO channels connected to node a, $B_a = \{b_{a1}, \ldots, b_{an}\}$. For each Kahn node, we define a computation requirement, shown with α_a, representing the computational workload imposed by that Kahn node onto a particular component in the architecture model. The communication requirement of a Kahn node is not defined explicitly, rather it is derived from the channels attached to it. We have chosen this type of definition for the following reason: if the Kahn node and one of its channels are mapped onto the same architecture component, the communication overhead experienced by the Kahn node due to that specific channel is simply neglected. Only its channels that are mapped onto different architecture components are taken into account. So our model neglects internal communications and only considers external communications. Formally, we denote the communication requirement of the channel b with β_b. To include memory latencies into our model, we require that mapping a channel onto a specific memory asks computation tasks from the memory. To express this, we define the computational requirement of the

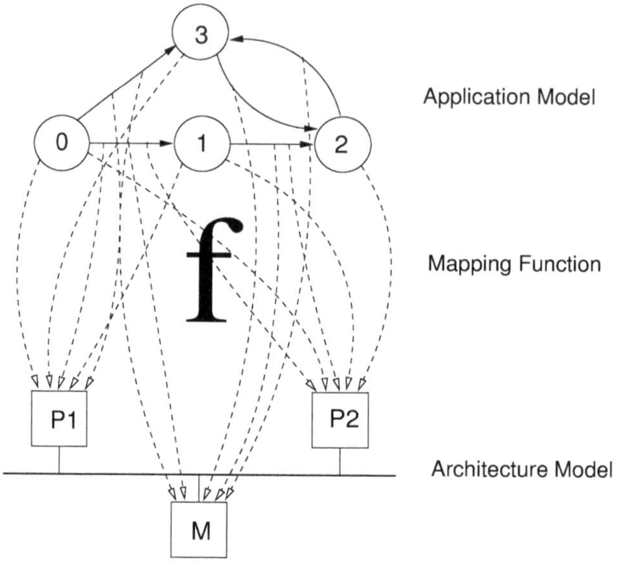

Figure 3.1: The mapping problem on a simple example. The mapping function has to consider multiple conflicting design objectives and should identify the set of Pareto-optimal mappings.

channel b from the memory as α_b. The formulation of our model ensures that the parameters β_b and α_b are only taken into account when the channel b is mapped onto an external memory.

3.2.2 Architecture modeling

Similarly to the application model, the architecture model is also represented by a graph $ARC = (V_A, E_A)$ where the sets V_A and E_A denote the architecture components and the connections between the architecture components, respectively. In our model, the set of architecture components consists of two disjoint subsets: the set of processors (P) and the set of memories (M), $V_A = P \cup M$ and $P \cap M = \emptyset$. For each processor $p \in P$, the set $M_p = \{m_{p1}, \ldots, m_{pj}\}$ represents the memories which are reachable from the processor p. We define processing capacities for both the processors and the memories as c_p and c_m, respectively. These parameters are set such that they reflect processing capabilities for processors, and memory access latencies for memories.

One of the key considerations in the design of embedded systems is the power consumption. In our model, we consider two types of power consumption for the processors. We represent the power dissipation of the processor p during *execution* with w_{pe}, while w_{pc} represents its power dissipation during *communication* with the external memories. For the memories, we only define w_{me}, the power dissipation during *execution*. For both processors and memories, we neglect the power dissipation during idle times. In our model, we also consider the financial costs associated with the architecture model components. Using an architecture component in the system adds a fixed amount to the total cost. We represent the fixed costs as u_p and u_m for the processors and the memories, respectively.

3.2.3 The mapping problem

We have the following decision variables in the model: $x_{ap} = 1$ if Kahn node a is mapped onto processor p, $x_{bm} = 1$ if channel b is mapped onto memory m, $x_{bp} = 1$ if channel b is mapped onto processor p, $y_p = 1$ if processor p is used in the system, $y_m = 1$ if memory m is used in the system. All the decision variables get a value of zero in all other cases. The constraints in the model are:

- Each Kahn node has to be mapped onto a single processor,

$$\sum_{p \in P} x_{ap} = 1 \qquad \forall a \in V_K. \tag{3.1}$$

- Each channel in the application model has to be mapped onto a processor or a memory,

$$\sum_{p \in P} x_{bp} + \sum_{m \in M} x_{bm} = 1 \qquad \forall b \in E_K. \tag{3.2}$$

- If two communicating Kahn nodes are mapped onto the same processor, then the communication channel(s) between these nodes have to be mapped onto the same processor.

$$x_{a_i p} x_{a_j p} = x_{bp} \qquad \forall b = (a_i, a_j) \in E_K. \tag{3.3}$$

- The constraint given below ensures that when two communicating Kahn nodes are mapped onto two separate processors, the channel(s) between these nodes are to be mapped onto an external memory.

$$x_{a_i p_k} x_{a_j p_l} \leq \sum_{m \in M_{p_k} \cap M_{p_l}} x_{bm} \qquad \forall a_i, a_j \in V_K, \quad \forall b \in B_{a_i} \cap B_{a_j}, \quad \forall p_k \neq p_l \in P. \tag{3.4}$$

- The following constraints are used to settle the values of y_p and y_m's in the model. We multiply the right-hand side of the first equation series by the total number of Kahn nodes and FIFO channels, since this gives an upper bound on the number of application model components that can be mapped to any processor. Similar logic is applied to the equations related with memory.

$$\sum_{a\in V_K} x_{ap} + \sum_{b\in E_K} x_{bp} \leq (|V_K| + |E_K|)y_p \quad \forall p \in P, \tag{3.5}$$

$$\sum_{b\in E_K} x_{bm} \leq |E_K| y_m \quad \forall m \in M. \tag{3.6}$$

Three conflicting objective functions exist in the optimization problem:

- The first objective function tries to minimize the maximum processing time in the system. For each processor and memory, f_p and f_m represent the total processing time of the processor and memory, respectively. We also show the total time spent by the processor for the execution events as f_p^e and for the communication events as f_p^c.

$$f_p = f_p^e + f_p^c, \tag{3.7}$$

$$f_p^e = \frac{1}{c_p} \sum_{a\in V_K} \alpha_a x_{ap}, \tag{3.8}$$

$$f_p^c = \frac{1}{c_p} \sum_{a\in V_K} x_{ap} \sum_{b\in B_a, m\in M_p} \beta_b x_{bm}, \tag{3.9}$$

$$f_m = \frac{1}{c_m} \sum_{b\in E_K} \alpha_b x_{bm}. \tag{3.10}$$

So the objective function is expressed as

$$\min \max_{i\in V_A} f_i. \tag{3.11}$$

- The second objective function tries to minimize the power consumption of the whole system. Similarly, g_p and g_m denote the total power consumption of processor p and memory m.

$$g_p = f_p^e w_{pe} + f_p^c w_{pc}, \tag{3.12}$$

$$g_m = f_m w_{me}. \tag{3.13}$$

$$\min \sum_{i\in V_A} g_i. \tag{3.14}$$

- The last objective function aims at minimizing the total cost of the architecture model.

$$\min \sum_{p\in P} u_p y_p + \sum_{m\in M} u_m y_m. \tag{3.15}$$

Definition 1 *Multiprocessor Mappings of Process Networks (MMPN) Problem is the following multiobjective integer optimization problem:*

$$\min \quad \mathbf{f} = (\max_{i \in V_A} f_i, \sum_{i \in V_A} g_i, \sum_{p \in P} u_p y_p + \sum_{m \in M} u_m y_m) \tag{3.16}$$

s.t. *(3.1), (3.2), (3.3), (3.4), (3.5), (3.6), (3.7), (3.8), (3.9), (3.10), (3.12), (3.13),*

$$x_{ap}, x_{bm}, x_{bp}, y_p, y_m \in \{0,1\} \qquad \forall a \in V_K, \ \forall b \in E_K, \ \forall m \in M, \ \forall p \in P. \tag{3.17}$$

For the sake of convenience Table 3.1 presents the set of mathematical symbols for the MMPN problem.

3.2.4 Constraint linearizations

In Section 3.4, we will solve an instance of the MMPN problem using both exact and heuristic methods. Because the problem has some nonlinear constraints, one has to linearize them before using a mathematical optimizer. Next we show how this is done.

(3.3) can be linearized by replacing it with these three constraints:

$$x_{bp} \geq x_{a_i p} + x_{a_j p} - 1, \tag{3.18}$$
$$x_{bp} \leq x_{a_i p}, \tag{3.19}$$
$$x_{bp} \leq x_{a_j p}. \tag{3.20}$$

Similarly, (3.4) can be linearized by introducing a new binary variable $x_{a_i p_k a_j p_l} = x_{a_i p_k} x_{a_j p_l}$ and adding the constraints:

$$x_{a_i p_k a_j p_l} \geq x_{a_i p_k} + x_{a_j p_l} - 1, \tag{3.21}$$
$$x_{a_i p_k a_j p_l} \leq x_{a_i p_k}, \tag{3.22}$$
$$x_{a_i p_k a_j p_l} \leq x_{a_j p_l}. \tag{3.23}$$

Finally, (3.9) can be linearized by introducing the binary variable $x_{apbm} = x_{ap} x_{bm}$ and adding the constraints:

$$x_{apbm} \geq x_{ap} + x_{bm} - 1, \tag{3.24}$$
$$x_{apbm} \leq x_{ap}, \tag{3.25}$$
$$x_{apbm} \leq x_{bm}. \tag{3.26}$$

3.3 Multiobjective optimization

3.3.1 Preliminaries

Definition 2 *A general multiobjective optimization problem with k decision variables and n objective functions is defined as:*

$$\begin{aligned} &\textit{minimize} && \mathbf{f}(\mathbf{x}) = (f_1(\mathbf{x}), \ldots, f_n(\mathbf{x})) \\ &\textit{subject to} && \mathbf{x} \in X_f \end{aligned}$$

Table 3.1: Table of symbols for the MMPN problem.

Application parameters	
V_K	set of Kahn nodes
E_K	set of channels
B_a	set of channels connected to node a
α_a	computation requirement of node a
β_b	communication requirement of channel b
α_b	computation requirement of channel b
Architecture parameters	
V_A	set of architecture components
E_A	connectivity set of architecture components
P	set of processors
M	set of memories
c_p	processing capacity of processor p
c_m	processing capacity of memory m
w_{pe}	power dissipation of p during execution
w_{pc}	power dissipation of p during communication
w_{me}	power dissipation of m during execution
u_p	fixed cost of p
u_m	fixed cost of m
Binary decision variables	
x_{ap}	whether a is mapped onto p
x_{bm}	whether b is mapped onto m
x_{bp}	whether b is mapped onto p
y_p	whether p is used
y_m	whether m is used
Functions	
f_i	total processing time of component i
g_i	total power dissipation of component i

where $\mathbf{x}$ *represents a solution and* $X_f \subseteq X$ *is the set of feasible solutions. The objective function vector* $\mathbf{f}(\mathbf{x})$ *maps a decision vector* $\mathbf{x} = (x_1, \ldots, x_k)$ *in decision space* (X) *to an objective vector* $\mathbf{z} = (z_1, \ldots, z_n)$ *in objective space* (Z)*.*

Definition 3 *(Dominance relations) Given two objective vectors* $\mathbf{z}^1$ *and* $\mathbf{z}^2$*, we say*

- $\mathbf{z}^1 \ll \mathbf{z}^2$ *(*$\mathbf{z}^1$ *strictly dominates* $\mathbf{z}^2$*) iff* $z_i^1 < z_i^2$, $\forall i \in \{1, \ldots, n\}$.
- $\mathbf{z}^1 < \mathbf{z}^2$ *(*$\mathbf{z}^1$ *dominates* $\mathbf{z}^2$*) iff* $z_i^1 \leq z_i^2$ *and* $\mathbf{z^1} \neq \mathbf{z^2}$, $\forall i \in \{1, \ldots, n\}$.
- $\mathbf{z}^1 \leq \mathbf{z}^2$ *(*$\mathbf{z}^1$ *weakly dominates* $\mathbf{z}^2$*) iff* $z_i^1 \leq z_i^2$, $\forall i \in \{1, \ldots, n\}$.
- $\mathbf{z}^1 \sim \mathbf{z}^2$ *(*$\mathbf{z}^1$ *is incomparable with* $\mathbf{z}^2$*) iff* $\exists i \neq j \in \{1, \ldots, n\}$ *such that* $z_i^1 < z_i^2$ *and* $z_j^2 < z_j^1$.

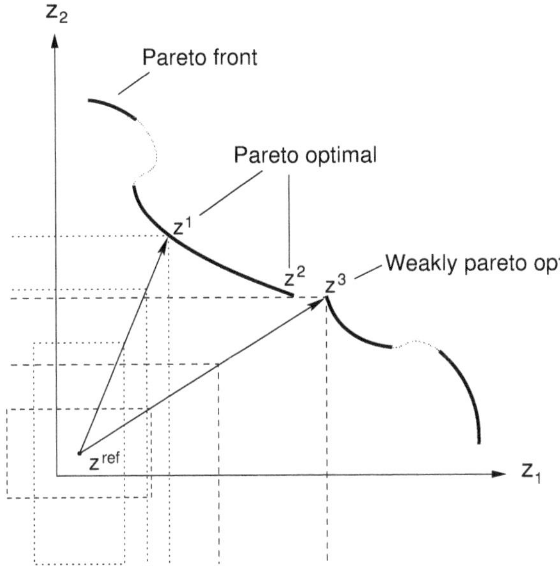

Figure 3.2: The lexicographic weighted Tchebycheff method can be considered as drawing probing rays emanating from $\mathbf{z}^{\text{ref}}$ towards the Pareto front. The points equidistant from $\mathbf{z}^{\text{ref}}$ form a family of rectangles centered at $\mathbf{z}^{\text{ref}}$.

Definition 4 *A decision vector* $\mathbf{x} \in A \subseteq X_f$ *is said to be nondominated in set* A *iff* $\nexists \mathbf{a} \in A$ *such that* $\mathbf{f}(\mathbf{a}) < \mathbf{f}(\mathbf{x})$.

Definition 5 *(Nondominated set and front) The set containing only nondominated decision vectors* $X_{nd} \subseteq X_f$ *is called nondominated set. Its image on the objective space,* $Z_{nd} = \{\mathbf{z} : \mathbf{z} = \mathbf{f}(\mathbf{x}), \mathbf{x} \in X_{nd}\}$ *is called nondominated front.*

Definition 6 *(Pareto set and front) The set* $X_{par} = \{\mathbf{x} : \mathbf{x} \text{ is nondominated in } X_f\}$ *is called Pareto set. Its image on the objective space* $Z_{eff} = \{\mathbf{z} : \mathbf{z} = \mathbf{f}(\mathbf{x}), \mathbf{x} \in X_{par}\}$ *is called Efficient set or equivalently Pareto front.*

Definition 7 *(Euclidean distance) The Euclidean distance between two vectors (of dimension* n*)* $\mathbf{z}^1$ *and* $\mathbf{z}^2$ *is defined as* $\|\mathbf{z}^1 - \mathbf{z}^2\| = \sqrt{\sum_{i=1}^{n} (z_i^1 - z_i^2)^2}$.

After these ground-laying definitions, in the rest of this section we first briefly explain an exact method for solving multiobjective optimization problems, namely the lexicographic weighted Tchebycheff method which was introduced by Steuer and Choo [92]. Then we will move to heuristic methods and introduce two state-of-the-art highly competitive Multiobjective Evolutionary Algorithms (MOEAs) [29], [109]. The discussion on MOEAs is performed within the context of the MMPN problem, especially when it comes to those problem specific parameters. We conclude this section by defining three new metrics for MOEA performance comparisons.

3.3.2 Lexicographic weighted Tchebycheff method

Definition 8 *(Weakly Pareto-optimal point) A solution* $\mathbf{x}^* \in X_f$ *is weakly Pareto-optimal if there is no* $\mathbf{x} \in X_{par}$ *such that* $\mathbf{f}(\mathbf{x}) \ll \mathbf{f}(\mathbf{x}^*)$.

The lexicographic weighted Tchebycheff method [92] works in two steps. In the first step, we take a reference vector in objective space with components

$$z_i^{\text{ref}} = \min\{f_i(\mathbf{x} \mid \mathbf{x} \in X_f)\} - \epsilon_i,$$

where ϵ_i are small positive values. Generally, it is common to set ϵ_i to the value which makes $z_i^{\text{ref}} = \lfloor \min\{f_i(\mathbf{x} \mid \mathbf{x} \in X_f)\}\rfloor$. In this step we solve

$$\begin{aligned} \min \quad & \alpha \\ \text{subject to} \quad & \alpha \geq \lambda_i |f_i(\mathbf{x}) - z_i^{\text{ref}}|, \\ & \sum_{i=1}^{n} \lambda_i = 1, 0 < \lambda_i < 1 \text{ and } \mathbf{x} \in X_f, \end{aligned} \tag{3.27}$$

which guarantees weak Pareto optimality [32]. We denote the set of solutions found in this first step with X_w. In the second step, solutions in X_w are checked for Pareto optimality using

$$\begin{aligned} \min \quad & \sum_{i=1}^{n} f_i(\mathbf{x}) \\ & \mathbf{x} \in X_w \end{aligned} \tag{3.28}$$

and all weakly Pareto-optimal points are eliminated. After this step, the retained Pareto-optimal solutions form X_{par}. In Figure 3.2, we illustrate this graphically. The first step in the lexicographic weighted Tchebycheff method can be considered as drawing probing rays emanating from $\mathbf{z}^{\text{ref}}$ towards the Pareto front. The points equidistant from $\mathbf{z}^{\text{ref}}$ form a family of rectangles centered at $\mathbf{z}^{\text{ref}}$. Moreover, the vertices of these rectangles lie in the probing ray in the domain of the problem [91]. The objective in (3.27) is optimized when the probing ray intersects the Pareto front. In this step, points $\mathbf{z}^1$, $\mathbf{z}^2$ and $\mathbf{z}^3$ can be located. In the second step, weakly Pareto-optimal $\mathbf{z}^3$ is eliminated.

3.3.3 Multiobjective evolutionary algorithms (MOEAs)

Evolutionary algorithms have become very popular in multiobjective optimization, as they operate on a set of solutions. Over the years, many multiobjective evolutionary algorithms have been proposed [21], [22]. In this section, we study two state-of-the-art MOEAs: SPEA2 which was proposed by Zitzler et al. [109] and NSGA-II by Deb et al. [29]. Both algorithms are similar in the sense that they follow the main loop in Algorithm 1. To form the next generation, they employ a deterministic truncation by choosing N best individuals from a pool of current and offspring populations. In addition, they both employ binary tournament selection [11]. Nevertheless, the main difference lies in their fitness assignment schemes.

Algorithm 1 A General Elitist Evolutionary Algorithm

Require: N: Size of the population
T: Maximum number of generations.
Ensure: Nondominated individuals in P_{t+1}.
step1. *Initialization:* Generate a random initial population P_0, and create an empty child set Q_0. $t \leftarrow 0$.
step2. *Fitness assignment:* $P_{t+1} \leftarrow P_t \cup Q_t$, and then calculate the fitness values of the individuals in P_{t+1}.
step3. *Truncation:* Reduce size of P_{t+1} by keeping best N individuals according to their fitness values.
step4. *Termination:* If $t = T$, output nondominated individuals in P_{t+1} and terminate.
step5. *Selection:* Select individuals from P_{t+1} for mating.
step6. *Variation:* Apply crossover and mutation operations to generate Q_{t+1}. $t \leftarrow t + 1$ and go to **step2**.

Despite the fact that both MOEAs apply a lexicographic fitness assignment scheme, objectives of which are to give first priority to nondominance and second priority to diversity, SPEA2 does so by using a finer-grained and therefore a more computationally expensive approach than its rival NSGA-II. The interesting question here is whether this additional computation effort pays off when we look at the overall performance of SPEA2 and NSGA-II. This issue is investigated experimentally in Section 3.4.

The distinctive characteristic of SPEA2 and NSGA-II is that both algorithms employ *elitism*, that is to guarantee a strictly positive probability for selecting at least one nondominated individual as an operand for variation operators. In both MOEAs, the following procedure is carried out to introduce elitism: the offspring and current population are combined and subsequently the best N individuals in terms of nondominance and diversity are chosen to build the next generation. Unlike single optimization studies, elitism has attracted high attention from the researchers in multiobjective optimization. Although it is still a very active research subject, elitism is believed to be an important ingredient in search with multiple objectives. For example in [61] and [108], experiments on continuous test functions show that elitism is beneficial, while in [107] similar results are also reported for two combinatorial (multiobjective 0/1 knapsack and travelling salesman) problems. Apart from these experimental studies, Rudolph has theoretically proven that an elitist MOEA can converge to the Pareto-front in finite number of iterations [84].

After the mentioned validatory studies, NSGA-II has been proposed as an elitist version of its predecessor NSGA. Besides elitism, NSGA-II has additional benefits over NSGA such as: i) a lower computational complexity, ii) a parameterless mechanism for maintaining diversity among nondominated solutions, iii) a deterministic selection algorithm to form the next generation by lexicographically sorting the combination of the current population and the offspring.

Similar to NSGA-II, SPEA2 is an improved successor of SPEA which was one of the first MOEAs with elitism. SPEA2 differs from SPEA in terms of i) a finer-grained fitness assignment mechanism, ii) a new density estimation technique for maintaining diversity, and iii) a new truncation method which prevents the loss of

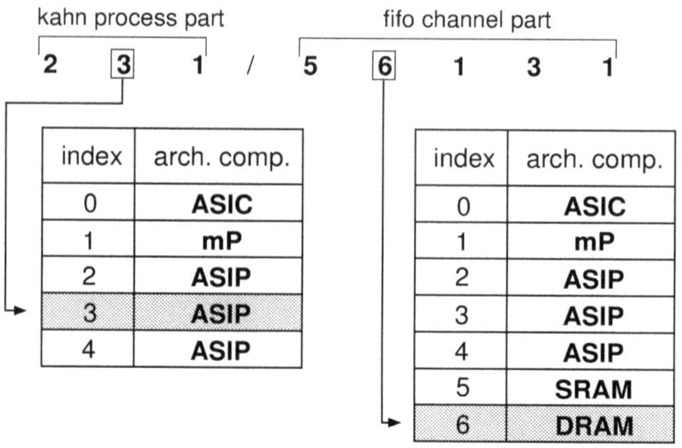

Figure 3.3: An example individual coding. The closely related genes are put together in order to preserve locality.

boundary solutions.

In the remainder of this section, we concentrate on problem-specific portions of MOEAs, and the discussion will be based on the MMPN problem, being our focus of interest in this chapter. The discussion is divided into three parts: individual encoding, constraint violations and variation operations. We conclude this section by defining three new metrics in the interest of comparing MOEAs under different criteria.

Individual encoding

Each genotype (i.e. representation of the possible mappings) consists of two main parts: a part for Kahn process nodes and a part for FIFO channels. Each gene in the chromosome (or genotype) has its own feasible set which is determined by the type of the gene and the constraints of the problem. For genes representing Kahn process nodes, only the set of processors in the architecture model form the feasible set, while for genes representing the (Kahn) FIFO channels, both the set of processors and the set of memories constitute the feasible set.

The constraints of the problem may include some limitations which should be considered in individual coding. For example, if there exists a dedicated architecture component for a specific Kahn process, then only this architecture component has to be included in the feasible set of this Kahn process.

In Figure 3.3, an example chromosome is given. The first three genes are those for Kahn process nodes, and the rest are those for FIFO channels. We have placed closely related genes together in order to maintain *locality*. The latter is vital for the success of an evolutionary algorithm [46], [30]. For this gene, the second Kahn process is mapped onto an Application Specific Instruction Processor (ASIP) while the second FIFO channel is mapped onto a DRAM. We also see that the feasible sets for these two genes are different.

Algorithm 2 Individual Repair Algorithm

Require: I (individual)
Ensure: I (individual)
  for all Kahn process genes **do**
    check if it is mapped onto a processor from its feasible set.
    if mapping is infeasible **then**
      repair: map on a random processor from its feasible set.
    end if
  end for
  for all FIFO channel genes **do**
    $K_1 \leftarrow$ source Kahn process of the FIFO channel.
    $K_2 \leftarrow$ sink Kahn process of the FIFO channel.
    $P_1 \leftarrow$ processor that K_1 is mapped onto.
    $P_2 \leftarrow$ processor that K_2 is mapped onto.
    if $P_1 = P_2$ **then**
      repair: map FIFO channel onto P_1.
    else
      $M \leftarrow$ a randomly chosen memory from $M_{P_1} \cap M_{P_2}$.
      repair: map FIFO channel on M.
    end if
  end for

Constraint violations

We have developed a repair mechanism to deal with constraint violations, that is infeasible mappings. Due to randomness in MOEAs (in initialization, crossover and mutation steps), the constraints (3.1), (3.2), (3.3) and (3.4) are prone to violation. The repair mechanism given in Algorithm 2 first considers whether each Kahn process is mapped onto a processor from its feasible set, and if not, it repairs by randomly mapping the Kahn process to a feasible processor. After having finished processing the Kahn process genes, it proceeds along with the FIFO channel genes. For the latter, the repair algorithm simply checks for each FIFO channel whether the Kahn processes it is connected to are mapped onto the same processor. If this condition holds, then it ensures that the FIFO channel is also mapped onto that processor. If the condition does not hold, which means that the Kahn processes are mapped onto different processors (say, P_1 and P_2), it finds the set of memories reachable from both P_1 and P_2 (mathematically, $M_{P_1} \cap M_{P_2}$). Then it selects a memory from this set randomly and maps the FIFO channel onto that memory. However, it is interesting to note here that if $M_{P_1} \cap M_{P_2} = \emptyset$, then the problem itself may become infeasible[1]. Therefore, we exclude these architectures.

With respect to repair, we have developed and tested three strategies. In the first (*no-repair*) strategy none of the individuals is repaired during any step, all are treated as valid individuals during the optimization process. Once the optimiza-

[1] Although, it is possible to repair by mapping both the FIFO channel and one of the Kahn processes onto the processor that the other Kahn process is mapped onto, this would require the individual to re-enter repair as it may cause additional infeasibilities for other FIFO channels. In the worst case, this can be an infinite loop.

tion is finished, repair is applied to the invalid individuals, and all nondominated solutions are output. Although this approach does not sound very promising as it neglects infeasibility, it is included here for two reasons: the first reason is that some researchers have applied this strategy to multiobjective combinatorial problems and reported positive results [30]; and the second reason is to see the performance gain/loss when constraint handling is taken into account. In the second strategy, which we call *moderate-repair*, all invalid individuals are repaired at the end of each variation (step6 in Algorithm 1). This allows infeasible individuals to enter the mutation step. The latter may help to explore new feasible areas over unfeasible solutions. This is especially important for combinatorial problems in which the feasible region may not be connected. The last strategy we employ here is called *extensive-repair*, as it repairs all invalid individuals immediately after every variation step. Hence, all individuals entering mutation are feasible. The experimental results concerning the repair strategies are discussed in Section 3.4.

Variation operations

As we have already mentioned, experiments in Section 3.4 should give us some feedback about i) whether the finer-grained computationally-expensive fitness assignment in SPEA2 pays off, and ii) the effect of using different repair schemes (no-repair, moderate-repair and extensive-repair strategies). Therefore, we have fixed other factors that may effect MOEA performance. We have used only one type of mutation and crossover operations in all standard runs. For the former, we have used independent bit mutation (each bit of an individual is mutated independently with respect to bit mutation probability), while for the latter standard one-point crossover (two parent chromosomes are cut at a random point and the sections after the cut point are swapped) is employed.

Many researchers have reported comparative performance results on different crossover types and mutation for traditional EAs solving single objective problems [46], [87], [94]. Therefore, it may well be interesting to perform similar comparative experiments with some variation operators in the multiobjective case. In this respect, we have performed additional experiments in Section 3.4.2 for the comparison of different crossover operators and the effect of mutation usage.

In our analysis with respect to crossover operators we have compared the performance of the one-point crossover with that of the two-point and uniform crossover operators. In two-point crossover the individual is considered as a ring formed by joining the ends together. The ring is cut at two random points forming two segments, and the two mating parents exchange one segment in order to create the children. One should note that the two-point crossover performs the same task as the one-point crossover by exchanging a single segment, however is more general. Uniform crossover is rather different from both one-point and two-point crossover; two parents are selected for reproducing two children, and for each bit position on the two children it is randomly decided which parent contributes its bit value to which child.

3.3.4 Metrics for comparing nondominated sets

To properly evaluate and compare MOEA performances, one can identify three important criteria [28]:

- **Accuracy.** The distance of the resulting nondominated set to the Pareto-optimal front should be minimal.
- **Uniformity.** The solutions should be well distributed (in most cases uniform).
- **Extent.** The nondominated solutions should cover a wide range for each objective function value.

Unlike single objective optimization problems, where the single aim is to locate a global optimum without being trapped at local optima, multiobjective optimization requires multiple aims to be satisfied simultaneously. Besides the obvious accuracy criterion, that is locating a set of solutions being at minimal distant from the Pareto front, multiobjective optimizers also need to maintain a well distributed solution set (i.e. uniformity) for a more complete view of the trade-off curve and should catch boundary points (i.e. extent) for a better coverage of the objective space.

There has been some effort for measuring the performance assessments of MOEAs [108], [59]. Metrics, in general, can be classified as i) metrics evaluating only one nondominated set, ii) metrics comparing two nondominated sets, iii) metrics requiring knowledge of the Pareto-optimal set, and iv) metrics measuring single or multiple assessment(s).

In the rest of this section, we propose one metric for each of the three identified criteria. Due to the fact that every objective function scales independently, one should map the limits of the objective function values to a unique interval, before doing any arithmetic operation. Therefore, we first present normalization of vectors, before defining the performance metrics.

Normalization of vectors in objective space

To make calculations scale independent, we normalize vectors before doing any arithmetic. At the end of normalization, each coordinate of the objective space is scaled such that all points get a value in the range $[0, 1]$ for all objective values. Assume we have p nondominated sets, $Z_1 \dots Z_p$. First we form $Z = Z_1 \cup \dots \cup Z_p$. Then we calculate $f_i^{min} = \min\{f_i(\mathbf{x}), \mathbf{f}(\mathbf{x}) = \mathbf{z} \in Z\}$ and $f_i^{max} = \max\{f_i(\mathbf{x}), \mathbf{f}(\mathbf{x}) = \mathbf{z} \in Z\}$ which correspond to the minimum and maximum values for the ith coordinate of the objective space. Then we scale all points according to

$$\overline{f}_i(\mathbf{x}) = \frac{f_i(\mathbf{x}) - f_i^{min}}{f_i^{max} - f_i^{min}}. \tag{3.29}$$

We repeat this process for all coordinates, i.e. $i = 1 \dots n$. We show the normalized vector of a vector $\mathbf{z}$ as $\overline{\mathbf{z}}$. Similarly, the set of normalized vectors are shown as $\overline{Z}$.

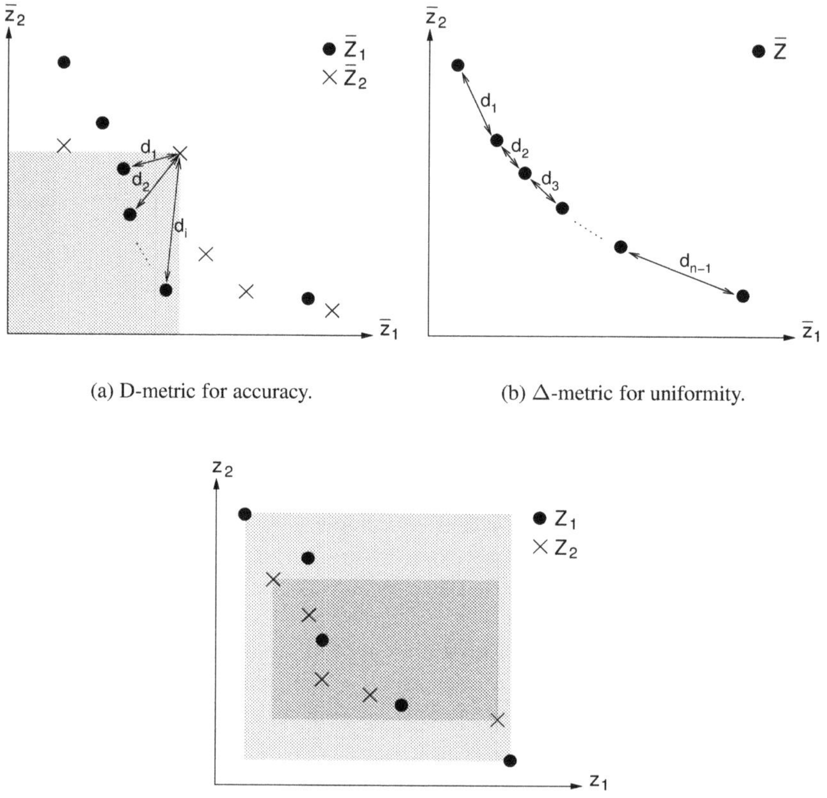

(a) D-metric for accuracy.

(b) Δ-metric for uniformity.

(c) ∇-metric for extent.

Figure 3.4: Metrics for comparing nondominated sets. For the sake of simplicity, illustrations for the two dimensional case are given. However, the metrics are also valid for any higher dimension.

D-metric for accuracy

Given two normalized nondominated sets $\overline{Z}_1$ and $\overline{Z}_2$, $\forall \bar{\mathbf{a}} \in \overline{Z}_1$ we look for $\exists \bar{\mathbf{b}} \in \overline{Z}_{21} \subseteq \overline{Z}_2$ such that $\bar{\mathbf{b}} < \bar{\mathbf{a}}$. Then we compute Euclidean distances from $\bar{\mathbf{a}}$ to all points $\bar{\mathbf{b}} \in \overline{Z}_{21}$. We define $\|\bar{\mathbf{a}} - \bar{\mathbf{b}}\|_{max} = \max\{\|\bar{\mathbf{a}} - \bar{\mathbf{b}}\|, \bar{\mathbf{a}} \in \overline{Z}_1, \bar{\mathbf{b}} \in \overline{Z}_{21}\}$ to be the maximum of such distances. If $\overline{Z}_{21} = \emptyset$ then $\|\bar{\mathbf{a}} - \bar{\mathbf{b}}\|_{max} = 0$.

$$D(\overline{Z}_1, \overline{Z}_2) = \sum_{\bar{\mathbf{a}} \in \overline{Z}_1} \frac{\|\bar{\mathbf{a}} - \bar{\mathbf{b}}\|_{max}}{\sqrt{n}|\overline{Z}_1|}, \tag{3.30}$$

where n is the dimension of the objective space. The D-metric returns a value in the range $[0, 1]$ where a smaller value is better. As seen in Figure 3.4(a), the maximum distance from a dominating point is taken as a basis for accuracy.

Δ-metric for uniformity

Given a normalized nondominated set $\overline{Z}$, we define d_i to be the Euclidean distance between two consecutive vectors, $i = 1 \ldots (|\overline{Z}|-1)$. Let $\hat{d} = \sum_{i=1}^{|\overline{Z}|-1} \frac{d_i}{|\overline{Z}|-1}$. Then we have

$$\Delta(\overline{Z}) = \sum_{i=1}^{|\overline{Z}|-1} \frac{|d_i - \hat{d}|}{\sqrt{n}(|\overline{Z}| - 1)}, \tag{3.31}$$

where n is the dimension of the objective space. Note that $0 \leq \Delta(\overline{Z}) \leq 1$ where 0 is the best. The underlying idea is to first calculate the average distance between any two consecutive points, and then to check all distances and penalize with respect to the deviation from the average distance. In the ideal case, all distances $d_1, d_2, \cdots, d_{n-1}$ in Figure 3.4(b) are equal to each other and the metric gets a value of 0.

∇-metric for extent

Given a nondominated set Z, we define $f_i^{min} = \min\{f_i(\mathbf{x}), \mathbf{f}(\mathbf{x}) = \mathbf{z} \in Z\}$ and $f_i^{max} = \max\{f_i(\mathbf{x}), \mathbf{f}(\mathbf{x}) = \mathbf{z} \in Z\}$. Then

$$\nabla(Z) = \prod_{i=1}^{n} |f_i^{max} - f_i^{min}|, \tag{3.32}$$

where n is the dimension of the objective space. For this metric, normalization of vectors is not needed. As shown in Figure 3.4(c), a bigger value spans a larger portion of the hypervolume and therefore is always better.

3.4 Experiments

For the experiments we have taken two media applications and a platform architecture to map the former onto the latter. The first application is a modified Motion-JPEG encoder which differs from traditional encoders in three ways: it only supports lossy encoding while traditional encoders support both lossless and lossy encodings, it can operate on YUV and RGB video data (as a per-frame basis) whereas traditional encoders usually operate on the YUV format, and finally it can change quantization and Huffman tables dynamically for quality control while the traditional encoders have no such behavior. We omit giving further details on the M-JPEG encoder as they are not crucial for the experiments performed here. Interested readers are pointed to [80].

The second application is a Philips in-house JPEG decoder from [26]. Regarding this application, we only have the topology information but not the real implementation. Therefore, we have synthetically generated all its parameter values. Both media applications and the platform architecture are given in Figure 3.5. Although these two applications match in terms of complexity, the JPEG decoder has a more complex structure since its processes are defined at a finer granularity.

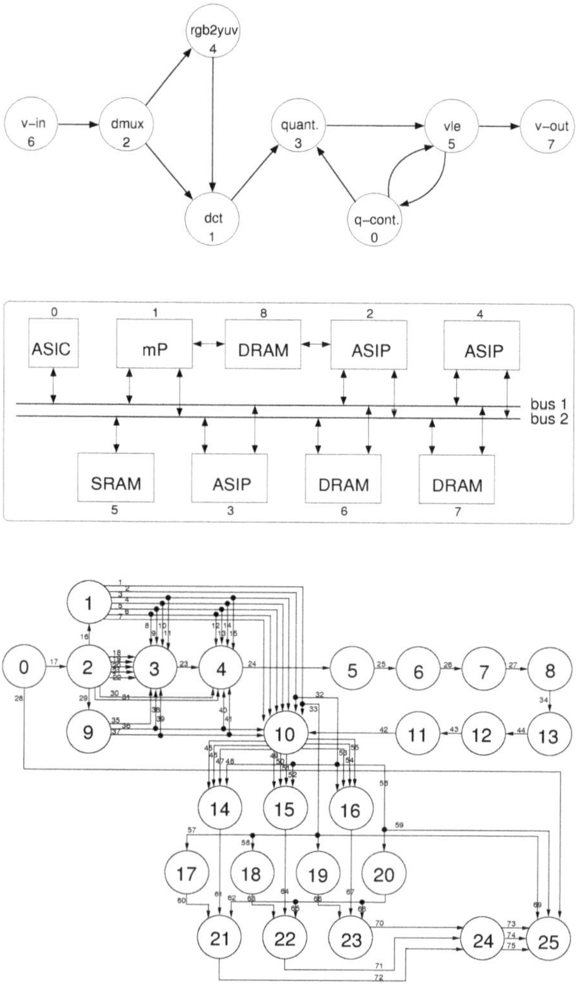

Figure 3.5: Two multimedia applications and a platform architecture is shown. The M-JPEG encoder application and the multiprocessor System-on-Chip (SoC) architecture model are given on the top; on the bottom is shown the JPEG decoder process network with 26 processes and 75 FIFO channels.

In two case studies performed here, we have mapped these media applications successively onto the same platform architecture consisting of a general purpose microprocessor (mP), three ASIPs, an Application Specific Integrated Circuit (ASIC), an SRAM and three DRAMs. For these architecture components, realistic latency values from [80] have been used to calculate their processing capacities: c_p and c_m. Similarly, for the Kahn processes and FIFO channels in the M-JPEG encoder, computational and communicational requirements (namely the parameters α_a for the

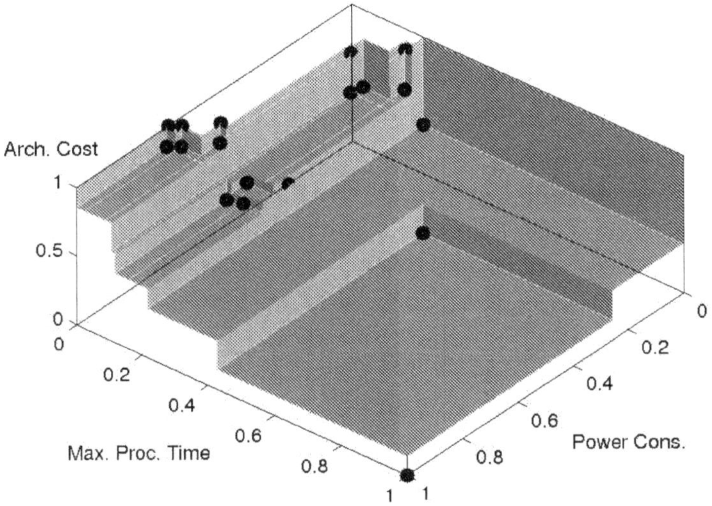

Figure 3.6: Pareto front for the M-JPEG encoder case study.

nodes and the parameters α_b and β_b for the FIFO channels) have been calculated using statistics obtained from the C++ implementation code of its Kahn process network.

We have implemented the MMPN problem as an optimization problem module in PISA – A platform and programming language independent interface for search algorithms [12]. In PISA, the optimization process is split into two modules. One module contains all parts specific to the optimization problem such as individual encoding, fitness evaluation, mutation, and crossover. The other module contains the problem-independent parts such as selection and truncation. These two modules are implemented as two separate processes communicating through text files. The latter provides huge flexibility because a problem module can be freely combined with an optimizer module and vice versa. Due to the communication via file system, platform, programming language and operating system independence are also achieved.

For the M-JPEG encoder and JPEG decoder mapping problems, we have utilized the state-of-the-art highly competitive SPEA2 and NSGA-II multiobjective evolutionary optimizers. As already mentioned in Section 3.3.3, we have used a repair algorithm (Algorithm 2) to handle constraint violations. In order to examine the effect of repair usage on the MOEA performance, we have utilized three different repair strategies (no-repair, moderate-repair, and intensive-repair), the details of which have already been discussed in Section 3.3.3. In the rest of the chapter we present the results obtained under the *no-repair* strategy with SPEA2 (NSGA-II), while the results for the *moderate-repair* and *intensive-repair* strategies are shown by SPEA2r (NSGA-IIr) and SPEA2R (NSGA-IIR), respectively.

In the experiments, we have used the standard one-point crossover and indepen-

Table 3.2: Experimental setup

MOEA	repair strategy	crossover	mutation
SPEA2	*no-repair*	one-point	indep. bit
SPEA2r	*moderate-repair*	one-point	indep. bit
SPEA2R	*intensive-repair*	one-point	indep. bit
NSGA-II	*no-repair*	one-point	indep. bit
NSGA-IIr	*moderate-repair*	one-point	indep. bit
NSGA-IIR	*intensive-repair*	one-point	indep. bit

dent bit mutation variators. The population size is kept constant. All performance analyses are carried out at different numbers of generations, ranging from 50 to 1000, collecting information on the whole evolution of MOEA populations. The following values are used for the specific parameters:

- Population size, $N = 100$.
- Maximum number of generations, $T = 50, 100, 200, 300, 500, 1000$.
- Mutation probability[2] 0.5, bit mutation probability[3] 0.01.
- Crossover probability 0.8.

The D-metric for measuring convergence to the Pareto front requires a reference set. To this end, we implemented the lexicographic weighted Tchebycheff method and solved the M-JPEG encoder mapping problem by using the CPLEX Mixed Integer Optimizer [25]. The outcome of numerous runs with different weights has resulted in 18 Pareto-optimal points which are plotted in Figure 3.6. The JPEG decoder is not solved by this exact method due to its size, instead the result obtained by running SPEA2 (with intensive-repair) for $T = 10,000$ is taken as the reference set.

Table 3.2 summarizes the experimental setup. In the experiments we have performed 30 runs (varying the random generator seed from 1 to 30) for each setup. An MOEA with some chosen T makes up a setup: SPEA2 with $T = 50$ or NSGA-IIR with $T = 500$ are two examples. As a result we have obtained 30 nondominated sets for each setup. All experiments have been performed on an Intel Pentium M PC with 1.7 GHz CPU and 512 MB RAM running Linux OS.

3.4.1 MOEA performance comparisons

Table A.1 in Appendix A presents averages and standard deviations of the three performance metrics for each experimental setup with respect to 30 runs. The results for the same number of generations are grouped and compared. The best

[2] i.e., the likelihood of mutating a particular solution.

[3] i.e., the likelihood of mutating each bit of a solution in mutation.

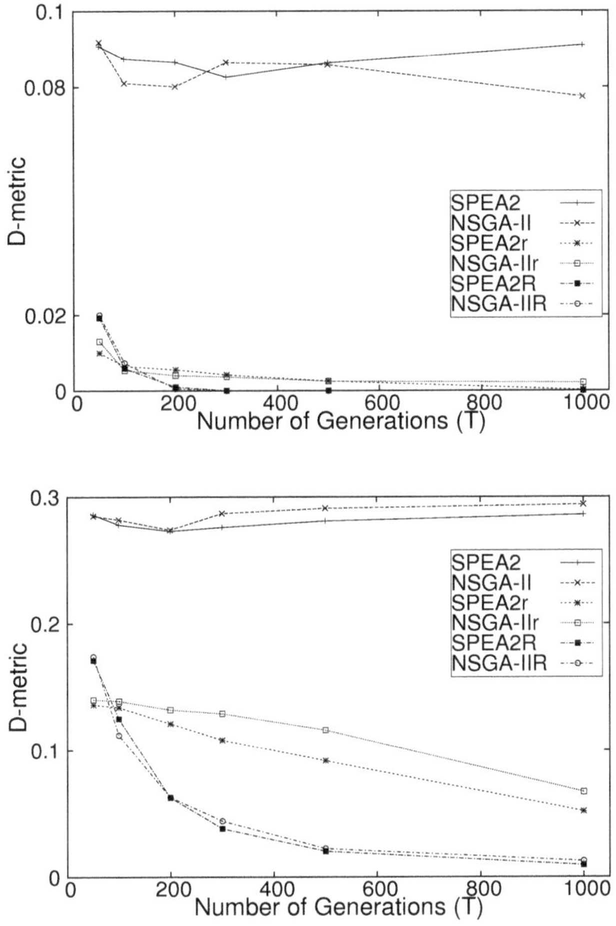

Figure 3.7: Convergence analyses of the D-metric for the M-JPEG encoder (up) and the JPEG decoder (down). In the case of the M-JPEG encoder, the reference set is obtained by CPLEX, while for the JPEG decoder it is obtained by running SPEA2r with $T = 10000$.

values obtained for all metrics are given in bold. To visualize the metrics convergence, we have plotted average metrics values against the numbers of generations in Figures 3.7, 3.8, and 3.9. We have the following conclusions:

- In terms of all three metrics, SPEA2 and NSGA-II score very close numbers and overall can be considered evenly matched. The same is true between SPEA2r and NSGA-IIr, and also for SPEA2R and NSGA-IIR. However with respect to run-times, NSGA-II, NSGA-IIr and NSGA-IIR outperform SPEA2, SPEA2r and SPEA2R by only demanding on average 44% of their rivals' run-times. The latter is also demonstrated in Figure 3.10 where we plot D-metric values with respect to wall clock time. Therefore, the

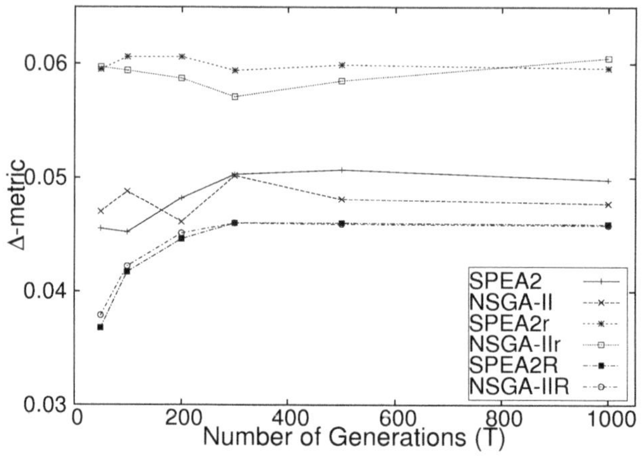

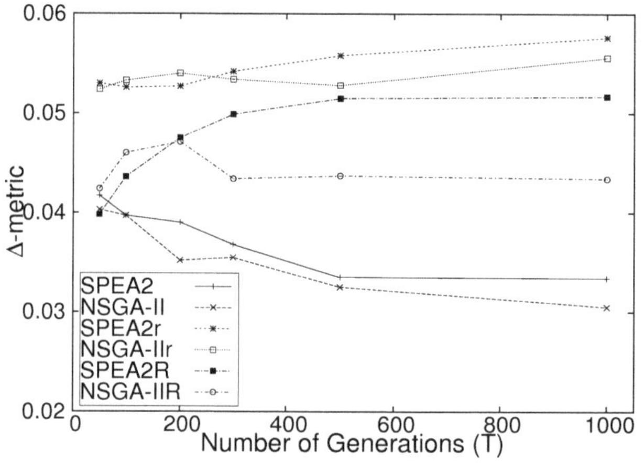

Figure 3.8: Convergence analyses of the Δ-metric for the M-JPEG encoder (up) and the JPEG decoder (down).

finer-grained computationally-expensive fitness assignment in SPEA2 (also in SPEA2r and SPEA2R) does not seem to pay off in general.

- In terms of accuracy (D-metric), SPEA2R and NSGA-IIR clearly outperform SPEA2r and NSGA-IIr. The worst performance is obtained when no repair is used, as clearly observed in Figure 3.7, SPEA2 and NSGA-II fail to converge to the Pareto front. Therefore, constraint handling is of crucial importance.

- From D-metric plots in Figure 3.7 and Figure 3.10 we observe that convergence to the Pareto front accelerates with higher usage of repair. In this respect we observe an exponential convergence curve for SPEA2R and NSGA-IIR, while the convergence of SPEA2r and NSGA-IIr approximates a linear

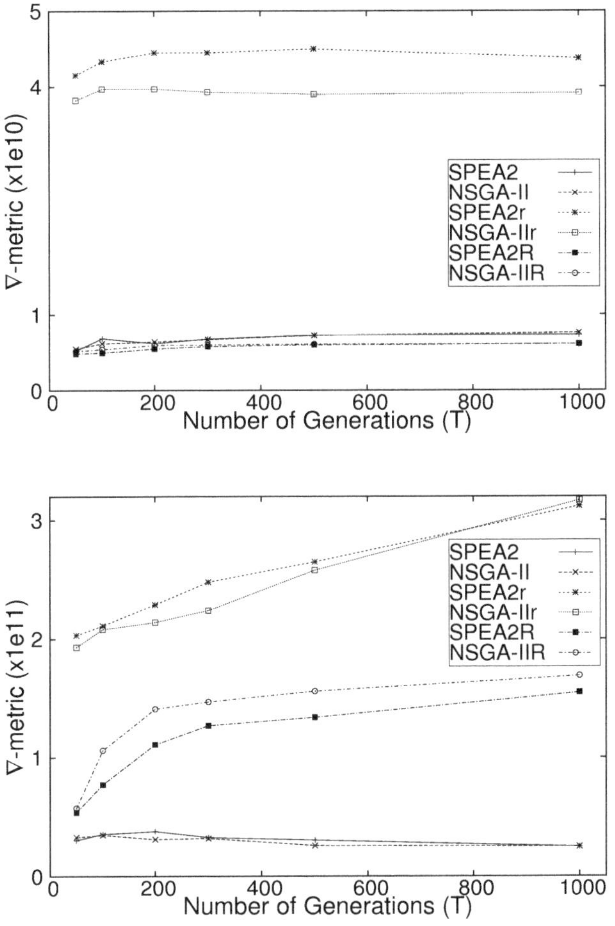

Figure 3.9: Convergence analyses of the ∇-metric for the M-JPEG encoder (up) and the JPEG decoder (down).

curve. However, as the number of generations increase, the difference in terms of D-metric between SPEA2R (NSGA-IIR) and SPEA2r (NSGA-IIr) diminishes.

- In terms of uniformity, all algorithms perform indifferently. Although they start from a good initial value, they all fail to converge towards the optimal value zero. It is also very difficult to come to any conclusion about their behaviors from Figure 3.8, e.g. it is unclear whether repair has any positive or negative effect on the Δ-metric. Overall, all algorithms can be considered as good in terms of uniformity, as they all score below 0.06 which is reasonably close to the optimal value.

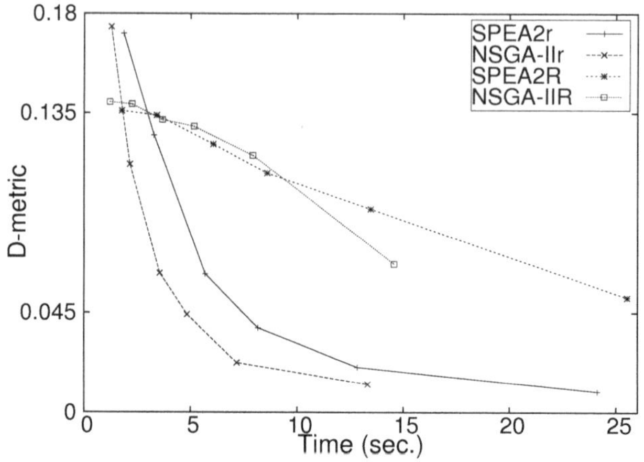

Figure 3.10: Convergence with respect to time.

- SPEA2r and NSGA-IIr clearly outperform other variants in terms of the extent metric. The reason behind this may be the higher explorative capacity of SPEA2r and NSGA-IIr, as they can locate diverse feasible regions by mutating the invalid individuals. In this metric, SPEA2R and NSGA-IIR come second. Also from the ∇-metric plot for JPEG decoder problem in Figure 3.9, we observe convergence behavior for SPEA2r, NSGA-IIr, SPEA2R, NSGA-IIR, but not for SPEA2 and NSGA-II. Therefore, repair is essential for good extension but there seems to be no linear relation between the two.

- In the M-JPEG encoder case study, we compare nondominated sets generated by the MOEAs against the exact Pareto set (obtained by the lexicographic weighted Tchebycheff method in CPLEX). As the numbers are very close to the ideal value 0 for $T \geq 300$, especially for SPEA2R and NSGA-IIR, we consider them as highly promising optimizers. Convergence to Pareto front is also achieved with SPEA2r and NSGA-IIr, but this takes considerably larger amount of time.

- In Figure 3.11 we perform reciprocal comparison of nondominated sets at numbers of generations 50, 100, 200, 300, 500, and 1000 for the JPEG decoder case study. To perform one comparison at a certain number of generations, 30 nondominated sets from an MOEA are compared one by one with the 30 nondominated sets from the other. The resulting distribution of 900 D-metric comparisons is given as a single notched boxplot in Figure 3.11. The comparisons unveil that SPEA2R and NSGA-IIR beat SPEA2r and NSGA-IIr in all comparisons; and SPEA2R and NSGA-IIR can be considered as equally matched. The same is true between SPEA2r and NSGA-IIr. However, as the number of generations increase, the difference in D-metric between SPEA2R (NSGA-IIR) and SPEA2r (NSGA-IIr) diminishes as a result of the belated convergence of SPEA2r and NSGA-IIr. This difference in convergence speed is also apparent in Figure 3.7, where we observe an expo-

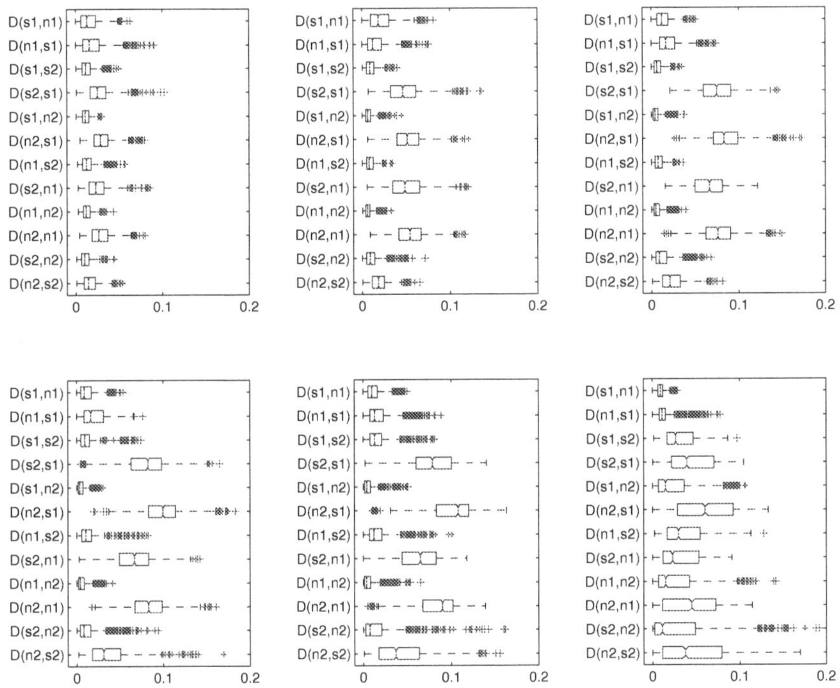

Figure 3.11: Notched boxplots showing the distribution of D-metric values for reciprocal comparison of MOEAs. Each nondominated set of a MOEA is compared with respect to each nondominated set from the other, and the resulting 900 comparisons is plotted. The plots are given for the JPEG decoder case study in ascending number of generations (50, 100, 200, 300, 500, and 1000) in the order from left to right and top to bottom. Hence, the top leftmost plot corresponds to MOEA comparisons with $N = 50$, while the bottom rightmost is for comparisons with $N = 1000$. The abbreviations s1, s2, n1, n2 are used in places of SPEA2R, SPEA2r, NSGA-IIR, NSGA-IIr, respectively. Comparisons regarding SPEA2 and NSGA-II are not given as they fail to converge (Section 3.4.1). Since D-metric is non-symmetric, i.e. $D(Z_1, Z_2) \neq D(Z_2, Z_1)$, both comparisons are performed. Note that smaller values are always better.

nential convergence curve for SPEA2R and NSGA-IIR in contrast to a linear curve for SPEA2r and NSGA-IIr.

3.4.2 Effect of crossover and mutation

In this section we have performed two independent experiments with the JPEG decoder case study in order to analyze the effect of crossover and mutation operators on different MOEA performance criteria. The purpose of the first experiment is to examine the correlation between crossover type and convergence to the Pareto front. In this respect, besides the default one-point crossover operator, we have

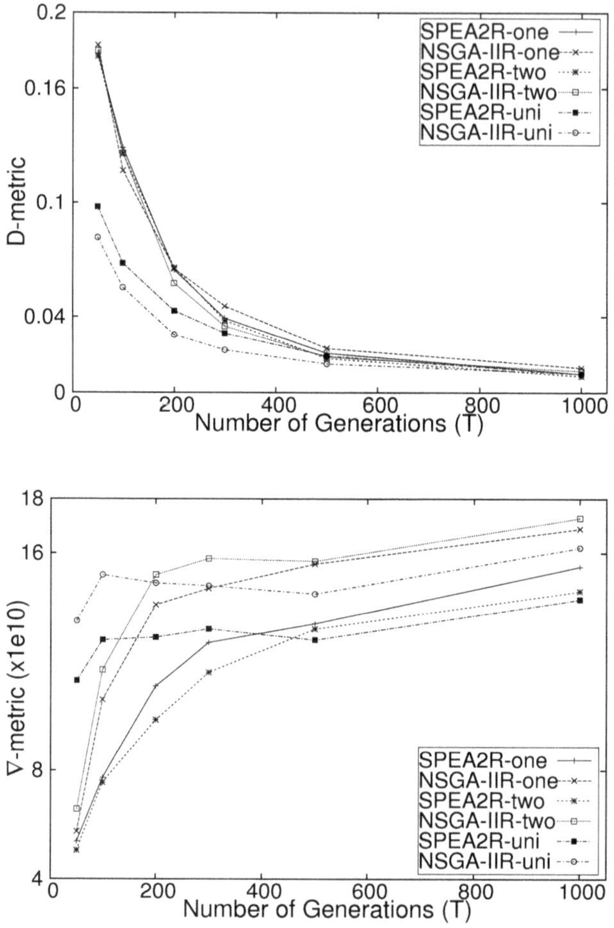

Figure 3.12: Crossover analysis for the JPEG encoder case study.

implemented two-point and uniform crossover operators (see Section 3.3.3 for how they work). When we look at the resulting D-metric plots in Figure 3.12 we observe a better performance with uniform crossover in the early generations; however after $T = 500$, all crossover operators exhibit very close performance. With respect to extent (∇-metrics in Figure 3.12) two point crossover shows the worst performance, while once again one-point and uniform crossover operators match each other. The relatively fast convergence but coincidentally poor coverage of the search space in the case of the two-point crossover implies that the operator is biased more towards exploitation than exploration. One-point and uniform crossover operators seem to find a better balance of the two in this case.

In the second experiment we analyze the effect of the mutation operator on MOEA performance. To realize this we have taken our original experimental setup

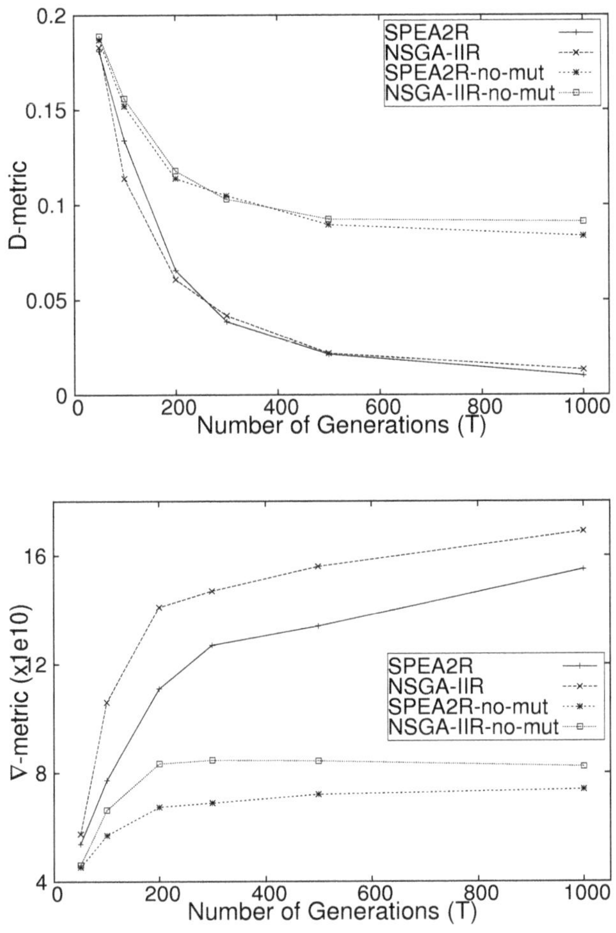

Figure 3.13: Using no mutation results in poor ∇-metric values in the JPEG encoder case study. This is an expected result as the mutation operator is responsible for exploration of the search space.

(see Section 3.4) and repeated the experiments without the mutation operator. The resulting D-metric and ∇-metric plots are given in Figure 3.13. With respect to both metrics omitting the mutation operator has resulted in very poor performance. MOEAs without mutation seem to converge towards the local optima and fail to collect variant solutions. Both observations imply that insufficient exploration has been realized in the search. These implications are in accordance with the widely accepted role of mutation as providing a reasonable level of population diversity in the standard EAs [87]. This experiment suggests that the explorative role of mutation is of high importance for MOEAs as well.

Table 3.3: Three solutions chosen for simulation.

Solution	Max. Processing Time	Power Cons.	Arch. Cost
cplex1	129338.0	1166.2	160.0
cplex2	162203.7	966.9	130.0
ad-hoc	167567.3	1268.0	170.0

3.4.3 Simulation results

In this section, we use the Sesame framework in order to evaluate three selected solutions of the M-JPEG encoder problem by means of simulation. Two of the solutions are taken from the Pareto-optimal set (referred here as cplex1 and cplex2), while the third solution is an ad-hoc solution (referred as ad-hoc) which is very similar to those proposed and studied in [65], [80]. It is clear from their objective function values in Table 3.3 that Pareto-optimal cplex1 and cplex2 outperform the ad-hoc solution in all objectives. The outcome of simulation experiments are also in accordance with optimization results (i.e. optimization results successfully estimate the correct trend), as the simulation results in Figure 3.14 reveal that similar performance can be achieved using less processing cores (cplex1 and cplex2 use three while ad-hoc uses four processors), which in turn results in less power consumption and cheaper implementation.

3.5 Conclusion

In this chapter, we studied a multiobjective design problem from the multiprocessor system-on-chip domain: mapping process networks onto heterogeneous multiprocessor architectures. The mathematical model for the problem takes into account three objectives, namely the maximum processing time, power consumption, and cost of the architecture, and is formulated as a nonlinear mixed integer programming. We have used an exact (lexicographic weighted Tchebycheff) method and two state-of-the-art MOEAs (SPEA2 [109] and NSGA-II [29]) in order to locate the Pareto-optimal solutions. To apply the exact method, we first linearized the mathematical model by adding additional binary decision variables and new constraints.

Three new performance metrics have been defined to measure three attributes (accuracy, uniformity and extent) of nondominated sets. These metrics are subsequently used to compare SPEA2 and NSGA-II with each other and also with the Pareto-optimal set. The two elitist MOEAs mainly differ in their fitness assignment schemes. SPEA2 uses a finer-grained and computationally more expensive scheme with respect to its rival NSGA-II. Performing two case studies, we have shown that SPEA2 is not superior than NSGA-II in any of the three defined metrics. Therefore regarding the MMPN problem, the computationally more expensive fitness assignment scheme of SPEA2 does not seem to pay off, as NSGA-II is on average 2.2 times faster. Comparing the two MOEAs with the exact set in the M-JPEG encoder case study, we have shown that both SPEA2 and NSGA-II find solution sets very

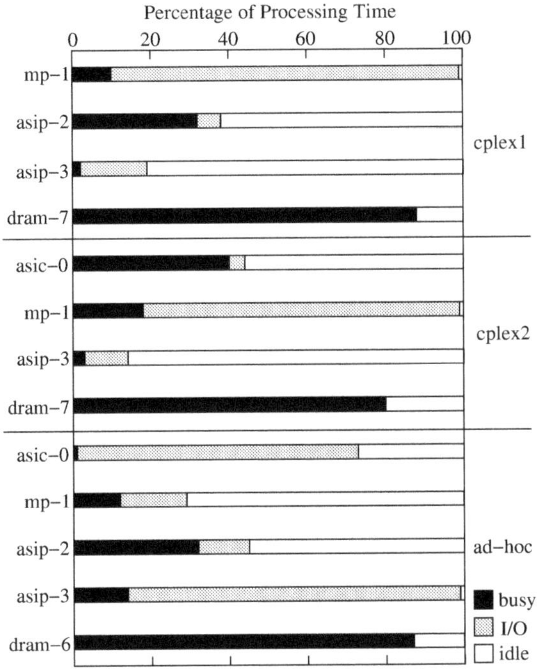

Figure 3.14: Simulation results showing the utilization of architecture components in all three solutions. The throughput values are 52.2, 47.8 and 51.3 frames/sec for the cplex1, cplex2 and ad-hoc solutions, respectively. As one should ideally target, in terms of trend behavior (not exact values), the throughput values from the simulations validate the optimization results given in Table 3.3.

close to the Pareto-optimal set.

Constraint violations have been tackled by three repair strategies differing in terms of repair intensity, and the outcome of each strategy is evaluated with respect to the defined metrics. The main result is that using sufficient amount of repair is necessary for good convergence, but allowing some infeasibility may help the MOEA to explore new feasible regions over infeasible solutions. Thus, a balance should be established in terms of repair frequency.

Additionally, one-point, two-point, and uniform crossover operators have been comparatively evaluated in terms of accuracy and extent. To summarize, one-point and uniform crossover operators seem to find a good balance of exploitation vs. exploration, while two-point crossover is more biased towards exploitation. With respect to mutation usage, the experiments reveal that mutation retains its importance for exploration.

We have also compared and simulated two Pareto-optimal solutions and one ad-hoc solution from previous studies [65], [80]. The results indicate that multi-objective search of the design space improves all three objectives, i.e. a cheaper implementation using less power but still performing the same in terms of system throughput can be achieved.

4

Dataflow-based trace transformations

We have seen in Chapter 2 that the Sesame simulation environment has a three layer structure: the application model layer, the architecture model layer, and the mapping layer which acts as an interface between the former two layers. The application model is composed of parallel Kahn processes, each executing sequential code and communicating with the other Kahn processes through first-in-first-out Kahn channels. Furthermore, the code of each Kahn process is annotated, which helps the process to record its actions when executed. Hence, when executed, each Kahn process emits a trace of application events which is often called the *application trace*. In general, there are three types of application events: *read* (R), *write* (W), and *execute* (E). The first two types of events stand for communication events while the last one is for computation events. These application events are typically coarse grained, such as *execute(DCT)* or *read(channel_id, pixel-block)*. In Sesame, the system-level performance evaluation of a particular application, mapping, and underlying platform architecture is performed by co-simulating application and architecture models via trace driven simulation. The mapping and architecture model layers simulate the performance consequences of the application events atomically (no interruptions are allowed during execution) and in strict trace order.

As design decisions are made, a designer typically wants to descend in abstraction level by disclosing more and more implementation details in architecture performance models. The ultimate goal of these refinements is to bring an initially abstract architecture model closer to the level of detail where it should be possible

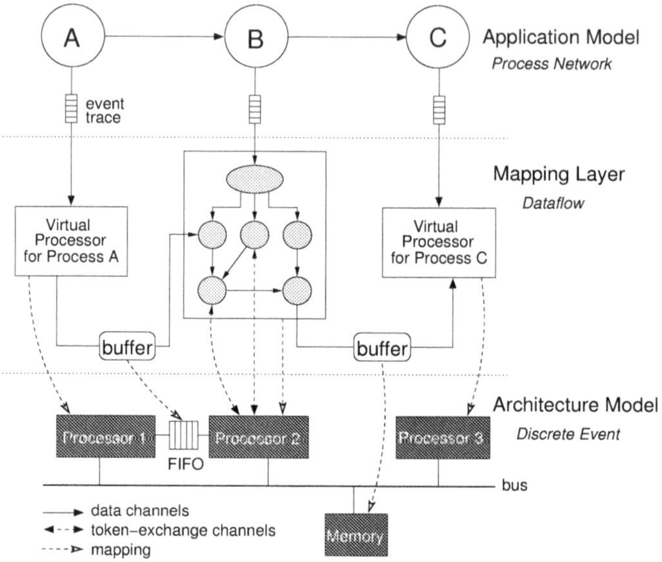

Figure 4.1: The three layers in Sesame: the application model layer, the architecture model layer, and the mapping layer which interfaces between the former two layers.

to synthesize an implementation. However, refining architecture model components in Sesame requires that the application events driving them should also be refined to match the architectural detail. Because Sesame maintains application models at a high level of abstraction to maximize their re-use, rewriting new application models for each abstraction level is not desirable. Instead, Sesame bridges the abstraction gap between application models and underlying architecture models at the mapping layer.

To give an example, consider Figure 4.1, where Kahn process B is mapped onto Processor 2 at the architecture level. Now, suppose that Processor 2 operates at the pixel level, where one pixel block of data at the application level corresponds to 64 pixels at the architecture level. Also assume that Processor 2 has an internal memory of limited size which can store only 32 pixels. Hence, Processor 2 needs to read 32 pixels of data from its input FIFO, do some computation on it, and write the resulting data to the shared memory. Then, it should repeat the same for the remaining 32 pixels. Using coarse grained R and W application events which are simulated atomically, such a behavior at the architecture level cannot be modeled.

To allow for modeling more complex scenarios such as sketched above, the underlying architecture model usually needs to have more refined events, which are named *architecture events*. This is because the architecture model components (such as processors, memory elements etc.) often operate at lower abstraction levels than the Kahn processes (in the application layer) which are mapped onto them. Therefore, there is also need for a transformation mechanism that translates the coarse-grained application events into the finer-grained architecture events. Such transformations should be realized without affecting the application model, allowing different refinement scenarios at the architecture level while keeping the application model unaltered. The natural solution to this is to place the transformation mechanism in between the application and architecture models, that is, in Sesame's mapping layer. As shown in Figure 4.1, trace transformations which transform application event traces into (more refined) architecture event traces are realized by refining the virtual processor components in Sesame with Integer-controlled dataflow (IDF) [16] graphs. However, before going into details of IDF-based trace transformations, we first formalize traces and their transformations mathematically in the next section. Then in the following section, we proceed with explaining the new mapping strategy in Sesame which realizes the IDF-based trace transformations. More information on the dataflow actors utilized in the new mapping strategy is given in Sections 4.3 and 4.4. Finally, we conclude this chapter with an experiment on trace refinement, and subsequently with some final comments.

4.1 Traces and trace transformations

In this section, we model traces and trace transformations that concern communication refinement mathematically. Although, we only concern communication refinement here, similar formulations can easily be derived for any trace transformations to be defined by the system designer. We first develop a trace transformation technique similar to the one introduced in [66], and in the following sections, propose a dataflow based framework to realize these transformations within the Sesame simulation environment. We should note that some transformation rules to be defined in this section are different from those in [66], and some parts of the discussion are treated with more detail. We also add a few examples to improve the clarity of the approach. We now proceed with giving basic definitions and trace transformations for communication refinement.

Definition 1 *A trace operation is either an application event emitted by the application model or an architecture event consumed by the architecture model. Each trace operation has an operation type. An application trace operation can be of type read* (R)*, execute* (E)*, write* (W)*, whereas an architecture trace operation, in the case of communication refinement, can be of type check-data* (cd)*, load-data* (ld)*, signal-room* (sr)*, check-room* (cr)*, store-data* (st)*, signal-data* (sd)*, execute* (E)*.*

In general, architecture trace operations are more fine grained than application trace operations. The types of trace operations of interest in this chapter are given in Table 4.1.

Definition 2 *Let* $\mathcal{R}$ *be a binary (ordering) relation defined on the set of trace operations* $O = \{o_i : i \text{ is unique}\}$ *where* $o_i \mathcal{R} o_j = (o_i, o_j) \in \mathcal{R}$ *means* o_i precedes o_j*. The elements of* $\mathcal{R}$ *are ordered pairs with* $\mathcal{R} \subseteq O^2$*.*

The ordering relation $\mathcal{R}$ is defined to have the following properties:

- $\mathcal{R}$ is reflexive, i.e. $\forall o_i \in O$, $o_i \mathcal{R} o_i$.

Table 4.1: Types of application and architecture trace operations.

Operation type	Operation	Event type information	Notation
Application	*read*	communication	R
Application	*execute*	computation	E
Application	*write*	communication	W
Architecture	*check-data*	synchronization	cd
Architecture	*load-data*	communication	ld
Architecture	*signal-room*	synchronization	sr
Architecture	*check-room*	synchronization	cr
Architecture	*store-data*	communication	st
Architecture	*signal-data*	synchronization	sd
Architecture	*execute*	computation	E

- $\mathcal{R}$ is antisymmetric, i.e. if $o_i \mathcal{R} o_j$ and $o_j \mathcal{R} o_i \Rightarrow o_i = o_j, \forall o_i, o_j \in O$.
- $\mathcal{R}$ is transitive, i.e. if $o_i \mathcal{R} o_j$ and $o_j \mathcal{R} o_k \Rightarrow o_i \mathcal{R} o_k, \forall o_i, o_j, o_k \in O$.

Lemma 1 *$\mathcal{R}$ is a partial order on O.*

Proof: Since the relation $\mathcal{R}$ is reflexive, antisymmetric and transitive, it is a partial order on O.

Throughout the rest of this chapter, we will use $\preceq$ to denote a partial order, and write $o_i \preceq o_j$ instead of $o_i \mathcal{R} o_j$ or $(o_i, o_j) \in \mathcal{R}$.

Definition 3 *A* trace $T =< O, \preceq>$ *is a partially ordered set (*poset*) defined on O with the relation $\preceq$. A trace with a total ordering is called a* linear trace.

When we draw a trace, we only draw the *base* of it defined by *Definition* 8. Thus, we never draw the reflexive property. Also an arc is not drawn if it is implied by the transitivity of the relation. That is, there is an arc from o_i to o_j if there is no other element o_k such that $o_i \preceq o_k$ and $o_k \preceq o_j$. The diagrams drawn in this manner are called *Hasse* diagrams.

Example 1 *Given an arbitrary trace $T =< \{a, b, c, d\}, \{(a, a), (a, b), (a, c), (a, d), (b, b), (b, d), (c, c), (d, d)\} >$, we draw its Hasse diagram as*

a → b → d
↘
c

Definition 4 *Assume we have a trace $T =< O, \preceq>$ with $x, y \in O$ and $x \preceq y$. We say y* covers *x in $\preceq$, if and only if there is no element $z \in O$ such that $x \preceq z$ and $z \preceq y$.*

Note that the above definition is closely related with the transitivity property. In fact, when we define the base of a trace below, we will eliminate all those pairs in $\preceq$ that makes it transitive.

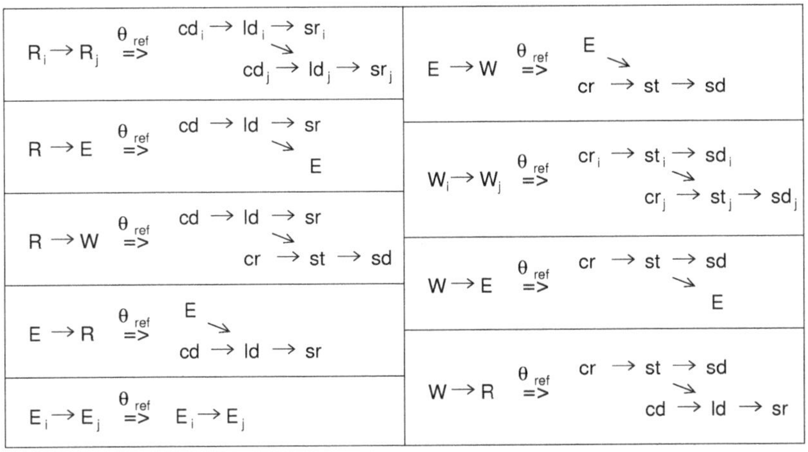

Figure 4.2: Trace transformation rules for communication refinement.

Definition 5 *The base of an ordering relation* $\preceq$ *is defined as* $\mathcal{B}(\preceq) = \{(o_i, o_j) : o_j$ *covers* $o_i\}$.

Generally, when we talk about a trace, we usually mean the base of it rather than itself. They are more useful, simple, and contain the same information. When we define transformations in the coming sections, we will define them on the bases.

Definition 6 *An* application trace T^{apt} *is a linear trace defined on the set of application operations* $O^{apt} = \{o_i : o_i \in APT\}$ *where* $APT = \{R, E, W\}$.

Example 2 *An application trace can be defined as* $T^{apt} =< \{R, E, W_1, W_2\}, \{ (R, R), (R, E), (R, W_1), (R, W_2), (E, E), (E, W_1), (E, W_2), (W_1, W_1), (W_1, W_2), (W_2, W_2)\} >$ *and it is drawn as* $R \rightarrow E \rightarrow W_1 \rightarrow W_2$.

Application-level operations *read*, *write*, and *execute* are shown as R, W, and E in the set of application operations O^{apt}, respectively.

Definition 7 *An* architecture trace T^{art} *is a linear trace defined on the set of architecture operations* $O^{art} = \{o_i : o_i \in ART\}$ *with* $ART = \{cd, ld, sr, E, cr, st, sd\}$.

We have defined both the application and architecture traces to be linear, i.e. totally ordered. For the application trace, this is because each Kahn process executes sequential code and consequently emits a linear trace. In the case of architecture traces, each Pearl object also consumes a linear trace. In Sesame, one can have processing components with multiple execution units which exploit task level parallelism. However, each execution unit is implemented by a separate Pearl object, and each object still simulates a single operation.

We define an architecture trace in the same manner we define an application trace. Only the working set contains architecture-level operations rather than application-level operations. Similarly, we use short terms for architecture-level operations in O^{art} and we abbreviate *check-data, check-room, load, execute, store, signal-room*, and *signal-data* as *cd*, *cr*, *ld*, E, *st*, *sr*, and *sd*, respectively. In this architecture trace, the application events capturing the communication (R and W type operations) are refined, but computation (E) events are left intact. However, later on in Section 4.5, we also show an example on computational refinement.

Example 3 *Returning back to Example 1, a trace was given as* $T =< \{a, b, c, d\}, \{(a, a), (a, b), (a, c), (a, d), (b, b), (b, d), (c, c), (d, d)\} >$, *now we write its base trace as* $B(T) =< \{a, b, c, d\}, \{(a, b), (a, c), (b, d)\} >$.

Definition 8 *A* trace transformation $\Theta(T)$ *is a mapping from one trace into another. It may change both O and $\preceq$ or only $\preceq$.*

Definition 9 (Communication refinement) *Let* $\Theta_{ref} : T^{apt} \rightarrow T^{int}$ *with* $O^{int} = \{o_i : o_i \in ART\}$ *be a linear trace transformation which maps a linear application trace onto a refined intermediate architecture trace. Linearity implies that* $\Theta_{ref}(T) = \Theta_{ref}(T_1) \rightarrow \Theta_{ref}(T_2) \rightarrow \ldots \rightarrow \Theta_{ref}(T_n)$ *where* $T = T_1 \rightarrow T_2 \rightarrow \ldots \rightarrow T_n$. *We now define a transformation rule for every ordered pair* (q_i, q_j) *of* O^{apt}, $q_i, q_j \in O^{apt}$. *Using these transformation rules, one can transform any application trace by making use of the linearity property.*

Trace transformation rules for communication refinement are given in Figure 4.2. These rules refine *read* and *write* events by making the data synchronizations explicit. Hence, in the case of an R event, the processor, onto which this Kahn process is mapped, first checks if the data is there (*cd* event), loads the data when it has arrived (*ld*), and finally signals that the data is read (*sr*). Similarly, a W is performed by the processor in three steps, which are represented by the *cr*, *st*, and *sd* events.

We should note that the synchronization operations *cd* and *cr* are blocking. This is because we implement a more restricted form of Kahn semantics at the architecture layer. Although Kahn channels are infinite in size at the application model layer, the corresponding FIFO buffers in the architecture model layer are finite in size. This enforces blocking write operations besides the usual blocking read operations from the Kahn semantics.

Example 4 *Suppose* $T^{apt} : R \rightarrow E \rightarrow W$ *is given. Find* $\Theta_{ref}(T^{apt})$. *We decompose* $T^{apt} = T_1 \rightarrow T_2$ *where* $T_1 : R \rightarrow E$ *and* $T_2 : E \rightarrow W$. *By linearity, we have* $\Theta_{ref}(T^{apt}) = \Theta_{ref}(T_1 \rightarrow T_2) = \Theta_{ref}(T_1) \rightarrow \Theta_{ref}(T_2)$. *Then, the transformation is*

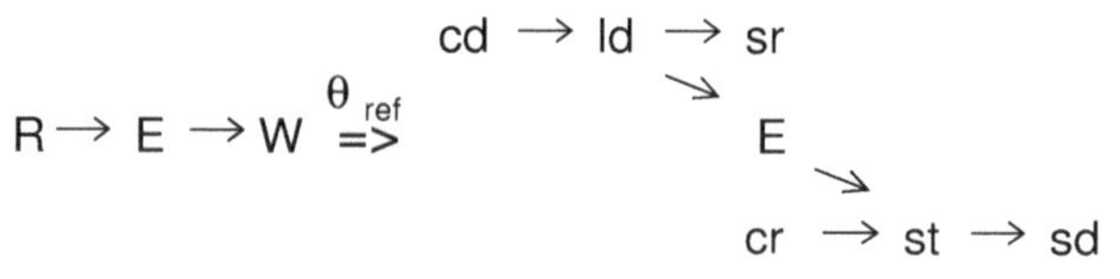

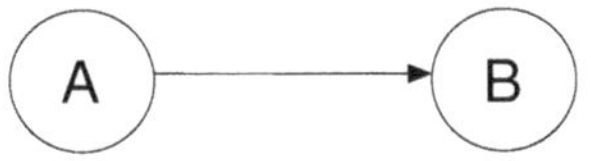


```
while(1) {        while(1) {
  write;            read;
  execute;          execute;
}                 }
```

Figure 4.3: Two Kahn processes in a pipeline.

Table 4.2: Operation priorities.

Arch. trace operation	Priority
check-data	*LOW*
check-room	*LOW*
load-data	*NORMAL*
store-data	*NORMAL*
execute	*NORMAL*
signal-data	*HIGH*
signal-room	*HIGH*

Definition 10 (Trace linearization) *The transformation $\Theta_{exec} : T^{int} \rightarrow T^{art}$ transforms an intermediate trace into an architecture trace for execution. The operations in the partially ordered intermediate trace are linearized (totally ordered) with respect to the priorities in Table 4.2, where ties are broken arbitrarily.*

The priorities in Table 4.2 are useful when one is given a partially ordered trace, which needs to be linearized for execution on a processor that accepts a linear trace. The idea behind these priority rules can be best explained with an example. Suppose that we have two Kahn processes in a pipeline each executing the sequential codes given in Figure 4.3. Hence, process A produces a trace of $W \rightarrow E$, while the execution of process B results in a trace of $R \rightarrow E$. We assume that processes A and B are mapped onto two processors P_1 and P_2, which execute linear traces, respectively. According to Figure 4.2, we have the following transformations:

The execution latencies for the refined events are given in the right side in Figure 4.4. For the sake of simplicity, we assume that the synchronization events only account time for pure synchronizations, events themselves take no processor cycles. On the left side in Figure 4.4, we plot the time diagrams (for each processor) corresponding to two cases where different architecture traces are executed by the processor P_1 onto which the process A is mapped. In both cases, the processor P_2 executes the refined trace which is linearized following the priority rules in Table 4.2. The time diagram given in the upper box is plotted for the case P_1 execute a trace linearized respecting the priority rules, whereas the one in the lower box is for the case in which the execution order of sd and E events are swapped. Time diagrams show the processor utilizations when three packets are processed in the pipeline. We observe that both processors are highly utilized when the priority rules in Table 4.2 are respected. These rules are the result of the following two intuitive rules: i) every processor should signal other processors (which may be waiting for this signal) in the system *as soon as possible* whenever it completes a task, ii) every processor should perform blocking operations (such as cd and cr), which may result in a stall in execution, *as late as possible*. We should anyway note here that these ordering rules are not strictly applied in Sesame. As we will later on see in this chapter, some trace linearizations can be performed in order to capture some

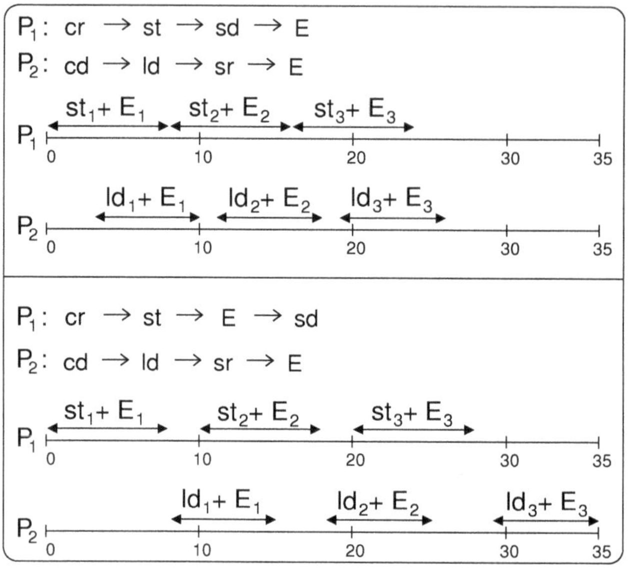

op.	lat.
cr	-
st	3
sd	-
E	5
cd	-
ld	2
sr	-
E	5

Figure 4.4: Example for trace execution.

processor characteristics, and these linearizations may as well violate the priority rules of Table 4.2. Besides, some processors can have more than one execution units which enable them to accept partially ordered traces for execution.

In Sesame, application traces produced by the Kahn processes are dynamically transformed into architecture traces in the mapping layer, and subsequently the transformed (architecture) traces are linearized and then executed by the processors in the architecture model layer. In the coming four sections, we present a new mapping methodology for Sesame which realizes these trace transformations within the co-simulation framework. According to this new mapping approach, the trace transformations are to be realized within the intermediate mapping layer, while the Kahn processes in the application model remain intact. The latter is an important property as it maximizes the re-usability of application models.

4.2 The new mapping strategy

Exploration environments making a distinction in application and architecture modeling need an explicit mapping to relate these models for co-simulation. As explained earlier in Chapter 2, in Sesame, we apply the trace driven (TD) co-simulation approach to carry out this task. To summarize it in short, the workload of an application, which is specified as a Kahn process network, is captured by instrumenting the code of each Kahn process with annotations. By executing the application model with specific input data, each process generates its own trace of applica-

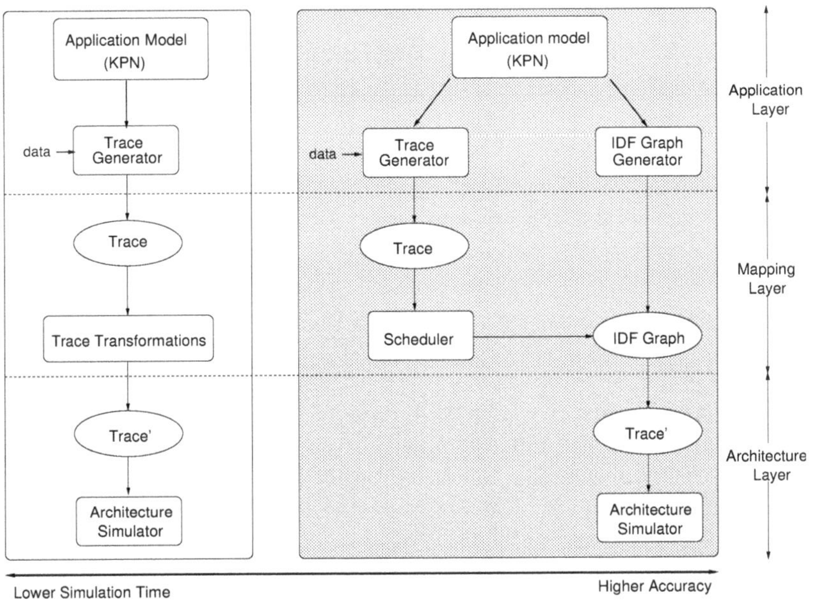

Figure 4.5: The traditional trace driven approach versus our enhanced trace driven approach.

tion events[1]. As we have already seen, these events are coarse-grained operations like *read(pixel-block,channel-id)* and *execute(DCT)*. At the mapping layer, *application traces* are transformed into *architecture traces* which are subsequently used to drive architecture model components. Such a trace transformation guarantees a deadlock-free schedule at the architecture layer when application events from different Kahn processes are merged. The latter may occur when multiple Kahn application processes are mapped onto a single architecture model component. Such a deadlock situation has already been given and further discussed in Section 2.4 of this thesis. This mapping strategy is illustrated on the left side in Figure 4.5.

Exploration environments using the TD approach can fail to provide numbers with high accuracy. This is due to the loss of application information (about control flow, parallelism, dependency between events, etc.) which is present in the application code, but which is not present in the totally ordered application traces. The Sesame environment, being a spin-off from the Spade project [67], also initially inherited its TD approach. Subsequent research on Sesame [77], [81] showed us that refining architecture model components also requires refining the architecture events driving them. Again due to the information loss in the application traces from which the architecture events are derived, the latter is not always possible with the traditional TD approach. The only way to improve this is to improve the mapping strategy. In Sesame, we make use of Integer-controlled Dataflow (IDF) graphs [16] at the mapping layer for this purpose. With the introduction of IDF

[1] In this thesis, we will use the terms (application/architecture) *events* and *operations* interchangeably throughout the text. They basically mean the same thing unless explicitly stated not to do so.

Table 4.3: A comparison of different mapping strategies.

Comparison criteria	TD	ETD	SP
Executable graphs	no	yes	no
Contain control flow information	no	yes	yes
Capture dependencies between events	no	yes	yes
Allow complex event transformations	no	yes	yes
Complexity of architecture models	low	low	moderate
Simulation time	low	moderate	moderate
Accuracy	low	high	high

graphs for mapping, we move from the traditional TD approach to a new mapping strategy which we call the Enhanced Trace Driven (ETD) approach [38].

This new mapping strategy, illustrated on the right side in Figure 4.5, can be explained as follows: for each Kahn process at the application layer, we synthesize an IDF graph at the mapping layer. This results in a more abstract representation of the application code inside the Kahn processes. These IDF graphs consist of static SDF actors (due to the fact that SDF is a subset of IDF) embodying the architecture events which are the – possibly transformed – representation of application events at the architecture level. In addition, to capture control behavior of the Kahn processes, the IDF graphs also contain dynamic actors for conditional jumps and repetitions. IDF actors have an execution mechanism called *firing rules* which specify when an actor can fire. This makes IDF graphs executable. However, in IDF graphs, scheduling information of IDF actors is not incorporated into the graph definition, and it should be supplied via a scheduler explicitly. The scheduler in Sesame operates on the original application event traces in order to schedule our IDF actors. The scheduling can be done either in a static or dynamic manner. In dynamic scheduling, the application and architecture models are co-simulated using a UNIX IPC-based interface to communicate events from the application model to the scheduler. As a consequence, the scheduler only operates on a window of application events which implies that the IDF graphs cannot be analyzed at compile-time. This means that, for example, it is not possible to decide at compile-time whether an IDF graph will complete its execution in finite-time; or whether the execution can be performed with bounded memory[2].

Alternatively, we can also schedule the IDF actors in a semi-static manner. To do so, the application model should first generate the entire application traces and store them into trace files (if their size permits this) prior to the architectural simulation. This static scheduling mechanism is a well-known technique in Ptolemy and has been proven to be very useful for system simulation [16]. However in Sesame, it does not yield to a fully static scheduling. This is because of the fact that the SDF actors in our IDF graphs are tightly coupled with the architecture model compo-

[2]Many of the analysis problems in IDF converge to the halting problem of Turing machines. This is due to the power of the MoC. In [15], Buck shows that it is possible to construct a universal Turing machine with only using BDF actors (IDF is an extension of BDF, see [16]) together with actors for performing addition, subtraction and comparison of integers.

nents. As will be explained shortly in Section 4.3.3, an SDF actor sends a token to the architecture layer to initiate the simulation of an event. It is then blocked until it receives an acknowledgement token from the architecture layer indicating that the performance consequences of the event have been simulated within the architecture model. To give an example, an SDF actor that embodies a *write* event will block after firing until the *write* has been simulated at the architecture level. This *token exchange mechanism* yields a dynamic behavior. For this reason, the scheduling in Sesame is rather semi-static.

In a closely related project Archer [110], Control Data Flow Graphs (CDFG) [103] are utilized for mapping. However, the CDFG notation is too complex for exploration, so they move to a higher abstraction level called Symbolic Programs (SP). SPs are CDFG-like representations of Kahn processes. They contain control constructs like CDFGs, however unlike CDFGs, they are not directly executable. They need extra information for execution which is supplied in terms of *control traces*. These control traces (which are somewhat similar to the traces we use) are generated by running the application with a particular set of data. At the architecture layer, SPs are executed with the control traces to generate architecture traces which are subsequently used to drive the resources in the architecture model.

In Table 4.3, we give a comparison chart for the three mapping strategies: TD, SP, and Enhanced Trace Driven (ETD). From this table, the advantages of ETD over TD should be clear as the former retains the application information that has been lost in the TD approach. This means that at the cost of a small increase of complexity at the mapping layer (and possibly a slight increase of simulation time) we now have the capability of performing accurate simulations as well as performing complex transformations (e.g. refinement) on application events. Comparing ETD to the SP approach, we see that they both allow for accurate simulations. In the ETD approach, all the complexity is handled at the mapping layer while in the SP approach it is spread over the mapping layer and the architecture model layer. The control traces and the SPs are created and manipulated (e.g. transformed) at the mapping layer, while they are also directed to the architecture layer to generate the architecture traces that derive the architectural simulation. This mechanism results in having more complex architecture model components in the SP approach which may hamper the architectural exploration. We also observe another advantage of the ETD approach over the SP approach that the graphs in the former are inherently executable while in the latter are not. This facilitates relatively easy construction of the system simulation.

4.3 Dataflow actors in Sesame

In this section, we introduce IDF actors utilized in Sesame. But before doing that, we first give a short intermezzo on firing rules for dataflow actors, which will be useful later in this section when we introduce and discuss Sesame's dataflow actors. This section is followed with a complementary section on, given a Kahn process and a trace transformation, how to build IDF graphs which implement the transformation by refining the corresponding virtual processor of the given Kahn process.

4.3.1 Firing rules for dataflow actors

A dataflow actor with $p \geq 0$ inputs can have N firing rules [63]

$$\mathrm{R} = \{\mathbf{R}_1, \mathbf{R}_2, \ldots, \mathbf{R}_N\}. \tag{4.1}$$

The actor is said to be *enabled* when at least one of the firing rules is satisfied. An actor can fire once it is enabled. A firing actor consumes input tokens and produces output tokens. Each firing rule contains a (finite) sequence called *pattern* for every input of the actor,

$$\mathbf{R}_i = \{R_{i,1}, R_{i,2}, \ldots, R_{i,p}\}. \tag{4.2}$$

For a firing rule $\mathbf{R}_i$ to be satisfied, each input stream j of the actor should contain $R_{i,j}$ as a prefix. By definition, an actor with no inputs is always enabled.

An empty stream is shown as $\perp$. In firing rules, some patterns may be empty streams, $R_{i,j} = \perp$, which means every stream at input j is acceptable and no token is consumed from that input when the actor fires. The symbol "$*$" denotes a token wildcard, i.e. $[*]$ shows a sequence with a single token (regardless of the type of the token) whereas $[*, *]$ shows a sequence with two tokens. If an actor consumes tokens from a specific input, the pattern for that input is of the form $[*, *, \ldots, *]$. If the type of the token is important, which is generally the case for control inputs, it is explicitly written in the firing rules. For example, a pattern like $[T]$ in a firing rule is satisfied when there exists a stream having a token of type T as the first element at the corresponding input.

Firing rules defined as a sequence of blocking read operations are known as *sequential firing rules* [63]. It can be shown that dataflow processes are continuous when the actors have sequential firing rules [63]. Since networks of continuous processes are determinate [54], dataflow process networks are determinate when every actor has sequential firing rules.

4.3.2 SDF actors for architecture events

Synchronous dataflow (SDF) [62] actors always have a single firing rule, which consists of patterns of the form $[*, *, \ldots, *]$, representing a fixed number of tokens, for each of its inputs. When an SDF actor fires, it produces a fixed number of tokens on its outputs, too. However, production of output tokens is not captured in the firing rules. Also not captured are the initial tokens which may be present on the inputs. Because an SDF actor consumes and produces a fixed number of tokens in each firing, it is possible to construct a schedule statically, which will transform the dataflow graph to its initial state after consecutive actor firings. Once such a schedule is found, it can be repetitively used to process streams of data tokens which are infinite in size. This property of SDF is important because embedded media applications process input data of unknown size that is practically considered to be infinite.

Figure 4.6 presents a simple SDF graph and a possible schedule (BAB) for this graph which fires actors in the order B, A, and B. The black dots on the channels

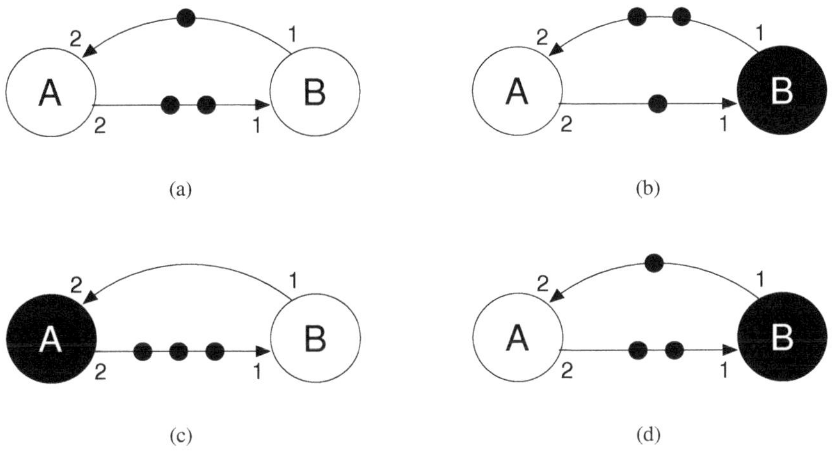

Figure 4.6: (a) A dataflow graph with two SDF actors. (b), (c), and (d) show a possible firing sequence (BAB) of actors which returns the graph to the initial state. With black dots on the channels are shown the initial tokens.

represent tokens being communicated over the channels. At the end of the firing sequence shown in Figure 4.6, the initial state of the graph is reached again, without any increase of tokens on the channels. The firing rules for the actors A and B are as $\mathrm{R} = \{[*, *]\}$ and $\mathrm{R} = \{[*]\}$, respectively. As shown in Figure 4.6, the numbers next to the inputs and outputs of an SDF actor represent the number of tokens it consumes or produces during firing.

To illustrate how SDF actors can be used to transform (i.e. refine) application events, consider the situation in Figure 4.7, where two Kahn processes (A and B) form a producer-consumer pair communicating pixel blocks. Let us further assume that Processor 1 in the figure produces lines rather than blocks, and four lines equal one block. Figure 4.8(a) illustrates the SDF graphs for the virtual processors A and B, which are the representations of the Kahn processes at the architecture layer. The virtual processor A refines the W(rite) application events from Kahn process A, which operates at the block level, with respect to the following transformation:

$$W \Rightarrow cd \rightarrow st(l) \rightarrow st(l) \rightarrow st(l) \rightarrow st(l) \rightarrow sd, \tag{4.3}$$

where $st(l)$ refers to a "store line". Since process A reads entire pixel blocks (ld in Figure 4.8(a)), synchronization occurs at the block level, that is, cr and cd events check for the availability of data/room of entire blocks.

The names of the actors in Figure 4.8(a) reveal their functionality. Some actors are represented by boxes rather than circles to indicate that they are composite SDF actors, which are explained in the next section. If no number is specified at the input (output) of an actor, then it is assumed that a single token is consumed (produced) at that input (output). Going back to virtual processor A in Figure 4.8(a), the cr actor fires when it receives a W(rite) application event and has at least one token on the

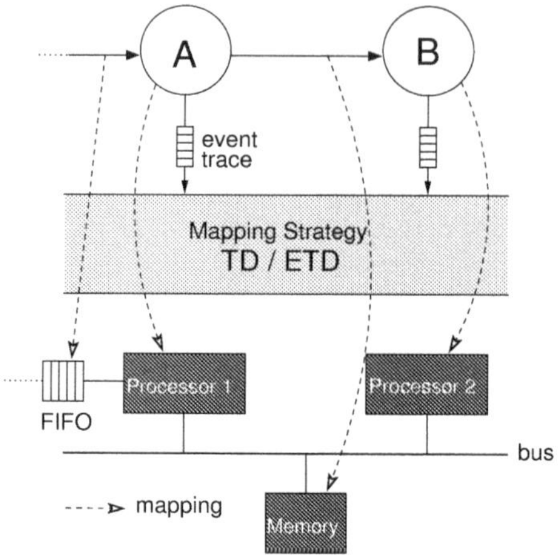

Figure 4.7: A possible mapping.

channel from the sr actor of virtual processor B. The number of tokens initially present on this channel, say b although shown only one in the figure, models a FIFO buffer of b elements between virtual processors A and B. Firing the cr actor produces four tokens for the $st(l)$ which subsequently fires four times in a row, where each firing produces a single token. Finally, the sd actor consumes four tokens when it fires, and produces a token for the cd actor in virtual processor B to signal the availability of a new pixel block. This means that we adopt *data-driven scheduling* in Sesame to schedule dataflow actors at the mapping layer, that is, all actors which can fire, i.e. all *enabled* actors, are always scheduled and fired in parallel in the first upcoming firing.

4.3.3 Token exchange mechanism in Sesame

An important feature of our SDF actors is that they can be coupled to architecture model components. In Sesame, SDF actors representing communication events such as R and W, or in case of communication refinement ld and st (but usually not synchronization events such as cd, cr, sd, and sr) and all computational events E are in fact composite SDF actors. Here, we should note that if one wants to account for the execution latency of the synchronization events, one could as well represent them with composite SDF actors. The structure of a composite SDF actor in Sesame is depicted in Figure 4.8(b). A composite SDF actor X is composed of two SDF actors X_{in} and X_{out}. When fired, the initial actor X_{in} sends a token to the architecture model which is represented by a dashed arrow in Figure 4.8(b). This token is typed, where the type information is used by the architecture model component to identify the event to be simulated. Once the performance consequences of the X event are simulated within the architecture model, an acknowledgement token is sent back to the X_{out} actor by the architecture simulator. The X_{out} actor can only fire when the acknowledgement token is received. Because SDF actors

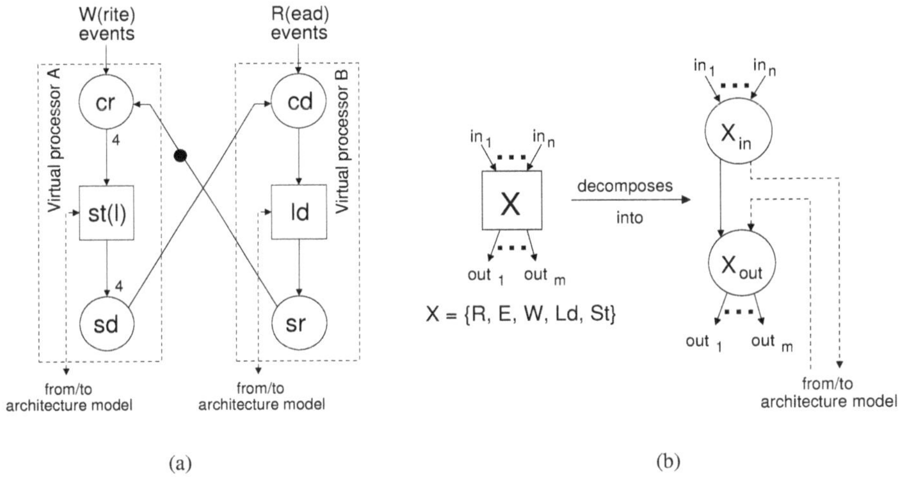

Figure 4.8: (a) Refining blocks to lines. (b) Composite SDF actors in Sesame which exchange tokens with the architecture model.

at the mapping layer and the architecture model components reside in the same Pearl simulation time domain (and thus share the virtual clock), the token transmission to/from the architecture model yields timed dataflow models. Hence, the time delay of, say an ld actor, depends on the ld event's simulation in the underlying architecture model. The same thing also holds for all composite SDF actors which represent other communication or computational events. Consequently, the scheduling in Sesame is semi-static (rather than static) due to the dynamic behavior introduced by the tightly coupling of the mapping and architecture layers.

Next, we introduce rest of the actors used in Sesame. This is followed by a discussion of the consequences of the new (dataflow based) mapping approach, and furthers examples on trace transformations for communication and computational refinements.

4.3.4 IDF actors for conditional code and loops

To properly handle conditional code and loops within Kahn processes, we use the IDF actors CASE-BEGIN, CASE-END, REPEAT-BEGIN, and REPEAT-END. These IDF actors have a special input which controls the behavior of the actor in execution. The IDF actor reads a typed token from this special input called the *control input*. The typed token carries a certain integer value, which is interpreted by the IDF actor to switch/select a certain input/output or to determine the number of repetitions.

The CASE-BEGIN actor in Figure 4.9(a), for example, reads an integer-valued token from its control input and then copies the first token on its data input to one

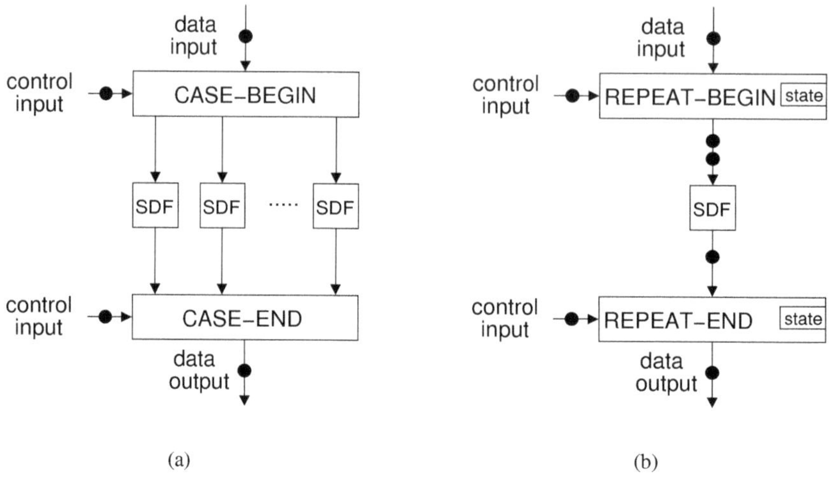

Figure 4.9: IDF actors for conditional code and loops. (a) CASE-BEGIN and CASE-END actors, (b) REPEAT-BEGIN and REPEAT-END actors.

of its output determined by the integer value. It has a single firing rule

$$\mathrm{R} = \{\{[*], [*]\}\}, \tag{4.4}$$

stating that when it fires, it consumes one token from its control and data inputs. Similarly, the CASE-END actor with p data inputs has p firing rules

$$\mathrm{R} = \{\{[*], \perp, \perp, \cdots, [1]\}, \{\perp, [*], \perp, \cdots, [2]\}, \cdots, \{\perp, \perp, \cdots, [*], [p]\}\}, \tag{4.5}$$

where the last sequence is written for the control input. Depending on the integer value of the control token, CASE-END consumes a single token from one of its inputs and produces a token on its output. It should be obvious that both CASE-BEGIN and CASE-END actors have sequential firing rules.

The multiphase REPEAT-BEGIN actor in Figure 4.9(b) has a starting phase which is followed by a series of execution phases. In its starting phase, the REPEAT-BEGIN actor consumes a single token from the data input and an integer-valued (typed) token from its control input. The length of the subsequent execution phases are determined by the control token. The state counter in the actor keeps track of the number of execution phases, i.e. the number of firings following the starting phase. The REPEAT-BEGIN actor produces a single token on its output in each of these subsequent firings. To show that the REPEAT-BEGIN is determinate, we have to include state information in the firing rules. By doing so, we add a third sequence representing the state of the actor in each firing rule. Consequently, we have $N+1$ firing rules for a multiphase REPEAT-BEGIN actor of cycle length N

$$\mathrm{R} = \{\{[*], [N], [*]\}, \{\perp, \perp, [1]\}, \cdots, \{\perp, \perp, [N]\}\}. \tag{4.6}$$

```
while(1) {
  read(in_NumOfBlocks, NumOfBlocks);
  // code omitted
  write(out_TablesInfo, LumTablesInfo);
  write(out_TablesInfo, ChrTablesInfo);
  switch(TablesChangedFlag) {
    case HuffTablesChanged:
      write(out_HuffTables, LumHuffTables);
      write(out_HuffTables, ChrHuffTables);
      write(out_Command1, OldTables);
      write(out_Command2, NewTables);
      break;
    case QandHuffTablesChanged:
      // code omitted
    default:
      write(out_Command1, OldTables);
      write(out_Command1, OldTables);
      break;
  }
  // code omitted
  for (int i=1; i<(NumOfBlocks/2); i++) {
    // code omitted
    read(in_Statistics, Statistics);
    execute("op_AccStatistics");
    // code omitted
  }
}
```

Figure 4.10: Annotated C++ code for the Q-Control process.

The starting phase, corresponding to $\mathbf{R}_1 = \{[*], [N], [*]\}$, resets the state counter, sets the cycle length N, and produces no output tokens. The multiphase REPEAT-END actor, on the other hand, consumes a data token on every execution phase, but produces an output token only on its final phase. It consumes a single token from its control input on the starting phase, and sets the state counter. The firing rules for a multiphase REPEAT-END actor of cycle length N can be similarly written as

$$\mathrm{R} = \{\{[*], [N], [*]\}, \{[*], \perp, [1]\}, \cdots, \{[*], \perp, [N]\}\}. \tag{4.7}$$

As before, the third sequence again corresponds to the actor state.

4.4 Dataflow actors for event refinement

In this section, we illustrate how we build IDF graphs with an example taken from the M-JPEG encoder application which we has been earlier introduced by Figure 3.5 in Chapter 3. In Figure 4.10, we present an annotated C++ code fragment of the Q-Control Kahn process at the application layer. The Q-Control process computes the tables for Huffman encoding and those required for quantization for each frame in the video stream, according to the information gathered about the previous video frame. This operation of the Q-Control process introduces *data-dependent* behavior into the M-JPEG application. In Figure 4.11, a corresponding IDF graph

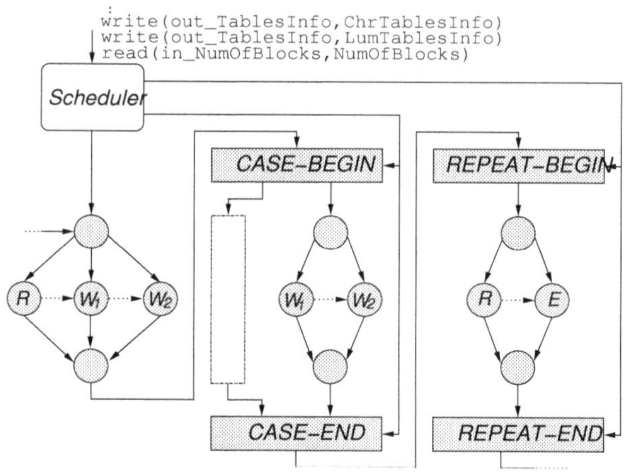

Figure 4.11: IDF graph representing the Q-Control process from Figure 4.10 that realizes high-level simulation at the architecture layer.

is given for realizing a high-level simulation. That is, the architecture-level operations embodied by the SDF actors (shown with circles) represent *read*, *execute* and *write* operations (shown as R, E, and W in Figure 4.11, respectively). These SDF actors drive the architecture layer components by the token exchange mechanism which was explained in Section 4.3.3. However, for the sake of simplicity, the architecture layer and the token exchange mechanism are not shown in the figure. As we already discussed in the previous section, the IDF actors CASE-BEGIN, CASE-END, REPEAT-BEGIN, and REPEAT-END model jump and repetition structures present in the application code. The scheduler reads an application trace, generated earlier by running the application code with a particular set of data, and executes the IDF graph by scheduling the IDF actors accordingly by sending the appropriate control tokens. In Figure 4.11, there are horizontal arcs shown with dotted lines between the SDF actors. Adding these arcs to the graph results in a sequential execution of architecture-level operations while removing them exploits parallelism. This is a good example that shows the flexibility of our mapping strategy.

In Figure 4.12, we present an IDF graph that implements *communication refinement* [77] in which communication operations, *read* and *write*, are refined in such a way that the synchronization parts become explicit. As explained in Section 4.1, an application-level *read* operation is decomposed into three architecture-level operations: *check-data*, *load-data*, *signal-room* (shown as cd, ld, and sr in Figure 4.12, respectively), and similarly, an application-level *write* operation is decomposed into three architecture-level operations: *check-room*, *store-data*, *signal-data* (shown as cr, st, and sd in Figure 4.12, respectively). The computational *execute* operations are not refined, they are simply forwarded to the architecture model layer. This type of refinement not only reveals the system-bottlenecks due to synchronizations, but also makes it possible to correct them by reordering the refined operations (e.g., early checking for data/room or merging multiple costly synchronizations). In this case, SDF actors represent these refined architecture-level operations. So, by sim-

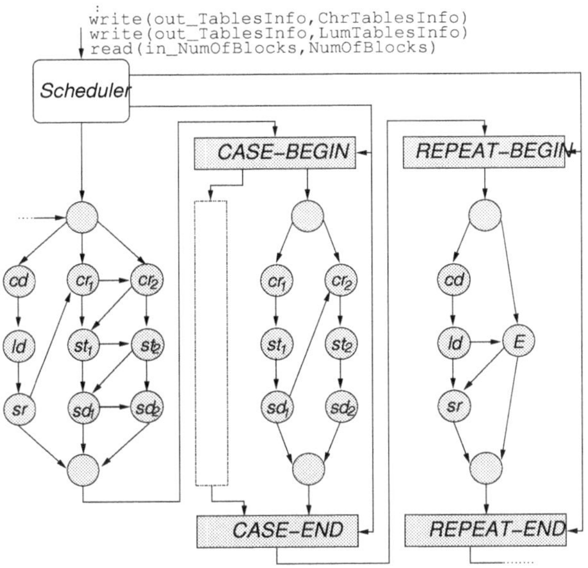

Figure 4.12: IDF graph for the process in Figure 4.10 implementing communication refinement.

ply replacing the SDF actors with the refined ones in a plug-and-play fashion, one can realize communication refinement (and possibly other transformations). Once again, the level of parallelism between the architecture-level operations can be adjusted by adding or removing arcs between the SDF actors.

We have also performed a simple experiment in which we explored how far the performance numbers of the TD (trace driven) approach diverge from the numbers of the ETD (enhanced trace driven) approach. The setup for the experiment is given by Figure 4.7. In this simple application, process A reads a block of data, performs a computation on it, and writes a block of data for process B. Simultaneously, process B reads a block of data and performs a computation on it. In this experiment, process A and process B are mapped onto Processor 1 and Processor 2, respectively. Processor 1 reads its input data from the dedicated FIFO while the communication between the two processors is performed through the shared memory. We consider the following scenario: we assume that Processor 1 has no local memory, thus before fetching data from the FIFO it should first consult the memory whether there is room for writing the results of the computation. This behavior requires the trace transformation

$$R \rightarrow E \rightarrow W \Rightarrow cd \rightarrow cr \rightarrow ld \rightarrow E \rightarrow st \rightarrow sr \rightarrow sd \qquad (4.8)$$

which enables Processor 1 to perform an early *check-room* and a late *signal-room*. The corresponding SDF graph (and also the alternative IDF graph) implementing this communication refinement is shown in Figure 4.13. Although an SDF graph is enough to implement this static transformation, an IDF graph implements it by a more simple graph with less channels. We modeled this behavior using the ETD

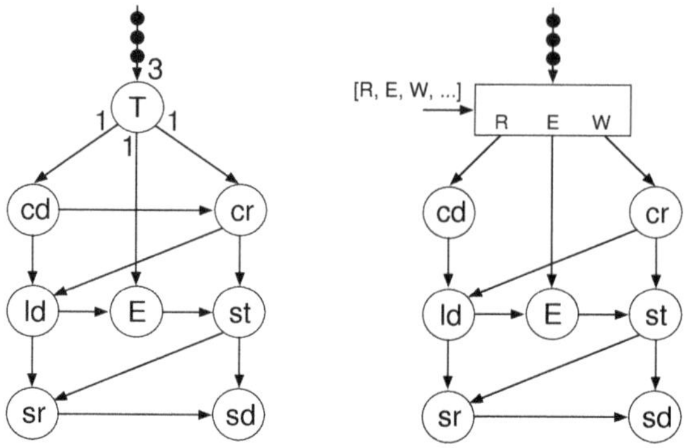

Figure 4.13: On the left SDF graph implementing the communication refinement in Equation 4.8 is shown. IDF graph for the same transformation is given on the right.

approach and compared our performance results with the numbers obtained by the TD approach.

Table 4.4: Error ratio matrix for the TD mapping approach.

		Speed of Processor 2			
		s	$2s$	$3s$	$4s$
Speed of Processor 1	s	44.6%	38.0%	29.7%	18.7%
	$2s$	40.4%	43.2%	34.3%	22.2%
	$3s$	32.4%	37.4%	40.7%	27.2%
	$4s$	21.8%	25.9%	31.8%	35.2%

In Table 4.4, we present how much the numbers of the TD approach deviate from the numbers of the ETD approach which models the correct behavior. We should note that we have performed 16 simulation runs using four different speeds for the processors, s being the slowest and $4s$ being the fastest. In Table 4.4, the values in rows (columns) are given for Processor 1 (Processor 2). From the simulation results we observe that the performance numbers obtained by the TD approach deviate between 18.7% and 44.6% from the correct numbers.

4.5 Trace refinement experiment

In this section, we are interested in refining grain sizes of both computation and communication events and subsequently model parallel execution (intra-task parallelism) of these events at the architecture level. More specifically, as our Kahn application models often operate on blocks of data, we look at the following trans-

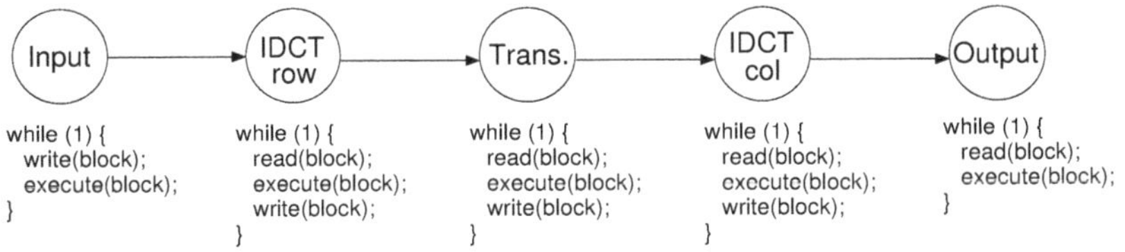

Figure 4.14: Kahn process network for the 2D-IDCT case study.

formations,

$$R \stackrel{\Theta}{\Longrightarrow} R(l) \rightarrow \ldots \rightarrow R(l), \tag{4.9}$$

$$E \stackrel{\Theta}{\Longrightarrow} E(l) \rightarrow \ldots \rightarrow E(l), \tag{4.10}$$

$$W \stackrel{\Theta}{\Longrightarrow} W(l) \rightarrow \ldots \rightarrow W(l), \tag{4.11}$$

$$E(l) \stackrel{\Theta}{\Longrightarrow} e_1 \rightarrow \ldots \rightarrow e_n \;. \tag{4.12}$$

In the first three transformations, read, execute and write operations at the block level are refined to multiple (e.g., 1 block = 8 lines) corresponding operations at the line level. We represent line level operations with an 'l' in parenthesis. The last transformation further refines execute operations at line level to model multiple pipeline execute stages inside a single processor. In (4.12), refinement for a processor with n-stage pipeline execution is given.

In Figure 4.14, a concrete example application model (a 2D-IDCT) is given to which the aforementioned trace transformations are applied. All the Kahn processes in the application model operate at block level, i.e. they read/write and execute operations on blocks of data. The Input process writes blocks of data for the IDCT-row process which in turn reads blocks of data, executes IDCT, and writes blocks of data. The Transpose process simply performs a matrix transpose to prepare data for the IDCT-col process.

We investigate two alternative architecture models for this application model, both given in Figure 4.15. Both architecture models have the same four processing elements, PE1 to PE4. The mapping of Kahn processes onto the processing elements is identical in both cases, they only differ in how these communicate. In the first architecture model, the PEs are connected via dedicated buffers while in the second architecture a shared memory is used. Each processing element is able to perform read, execute and write operations in parallel, so it can perform its task in a pipelined fashion. Input and Output processes are mapped onto PE1 and PE4, IDCT-row and IDCT-col are mapped onto PE2 and PE3, respectively. The Transpose process is not mapped onto anything, since its functionality is simply implemented as follows: the processing element on which the IDCT-row process is mapped simply writes rows of data to the memory while the processing element on which the second IDCT process is mapped reads columns of data from the memory. We should note that this type of implementation of the matrix transpose forces those processing elements, operating at line level (as we will explain later on in this section), to be synchronized at block level. This is because the second processing

(a)

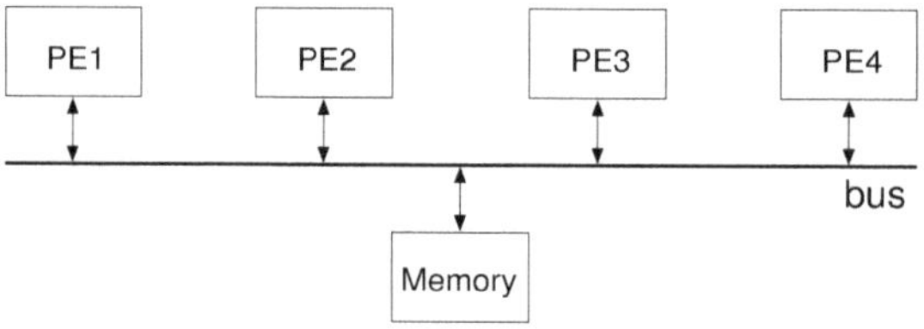

(b)

Figure 4.15: Two different target architectures.

element cannot start processing lines until the first one is finished with the last line of data.

In both architectures, we modeled PE1 and PE4 to operate at block level. We first modeled PE2 and PE3 to operate at the more abstract block level, and then later refined them to operate at line level. As shown in Figure 4.16(a), after refinement, PE2 and PE3 now have pipelined R, E, and W units. Due to this refinement, the application events from the IDCT processes need also to be refined. The pattern to be refined for the IDCT processes is $R \to E \to W$. For simplicity if we assume 1 block = 2 lines then,

$$R \to E \to W \overset{\theta_{ref}}{\Rightarrow} \begin{array}{llllll} R(l) \to & E(l) \to & W(l) & & & \\ & \searrow & \searrow & \searrow & & \\ & R(l) \to & E(l) \to & W(l) & & \end{array} \tag{4.13}$$

As shown in Figure 4.16(b), if we further define that PE2 and PE3 are processing elements with 2-stage pipeline execution units, which creates an execution pipeline inside the previously mentioned task pipeline, then from (4.12) with $n = 2$ we

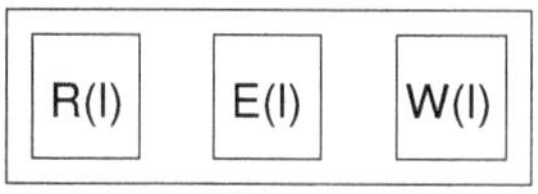

(a)

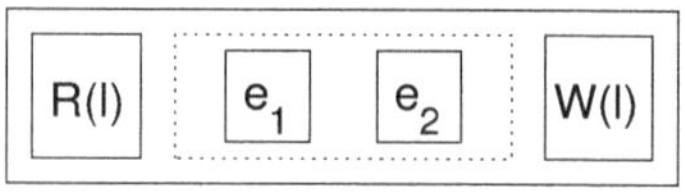

(b)

Figure 4.16: (a) PE2 and PE3 with pipelined R, E, and W units. (b) E unit is further refined to have more pipelined execution units.

Table 4.5: Parameters for simulation.

	Non-refined Shared	Refined Shared	Non-refined FIFO	Refined FIFO
Pipeline size	–	3/8	–	3/8
PE2, PE3 execution latency	300	13/5	300	13/5
PE2, PE3 data size	64	8	64	8
PE1, PE4 data size	64	64	64	64
FIFO latency	–	–	1 ... 60	1 ... 60
Memory latency	1 ... 60	1 ... 60	–	–
Memory width	8	8	–	–
Bus setup latency	1	1	–	–
Bus width	8	8	–	–

obtain,

$$R \rightarrow E \rightarrow W \overset{\theta_{ref}}{\Rightarrow} \begin{array}{l} R(l) \rightarrow e_1 \rightarrow e_2 \rightarrow W(l) \\ \quad \searrow \qquad \searrow \qquad \searrow \qquad \searrow \\ \qquad R(l) \rightarrow e_1 \rightarrow e_2 \rightarrow W(l) \end{array} \qquad (4.14)$$

In Table 4.5, we give the simulation parameters. We have performed four simulations represented by the four columns in the table. The terms *non-refined* and *refined* indicate whether the processing elements PE2 and PE3 operate at block level or at line level in our model. The terms *fifo* and *shared* refer to the architectures in Figures 4.15(a) and 4.15(b), respectively. Execution latency is measured in cycles, and data size in bytes. Memory and FIFO latencies are given in cycles/line, where 1 line is 8 bytes and 8 lines make up a block. We note that in these experiments the ratios between the parameters are more important than the actual values being used. We assume that executing a 1D-IDCT takes 300 cycles per block on a non-refined execution unit, so in a 3-stage pipelined execution unit operating on lines, the amount of work is divided by the number of stages, and by the number of lines in a block. So the execution latency of one stage in the 3-stage pipeline is 13 cycles and that of the 8-stage is 5 cycles.

In Figure 4.17, we give the performance graph obtained when we map the 2D-IDCT application onto the architectures in Figure 4.15. In all experiments, we have processed 500 blocks of input data. In the first experiment, the processing elements PE2 and PE3 operate at block level and no refinement is performed. This gives us performance results for single and double buffer implementations, i.e. where the double buffer is a 2-entry buffer so that the producer can write to it and the consumer can read from it, simultaneously. In the second experiment, we refined the processing elements PE2 and PE3 in the architecture model, and explored four alternative cases. For these two processing elements, we have used a 3-stage and an 8-stage execution pipeline.

For the buffers, we have again experimented with single and double buffer implementations. When we compare the single and double buffer performance of the

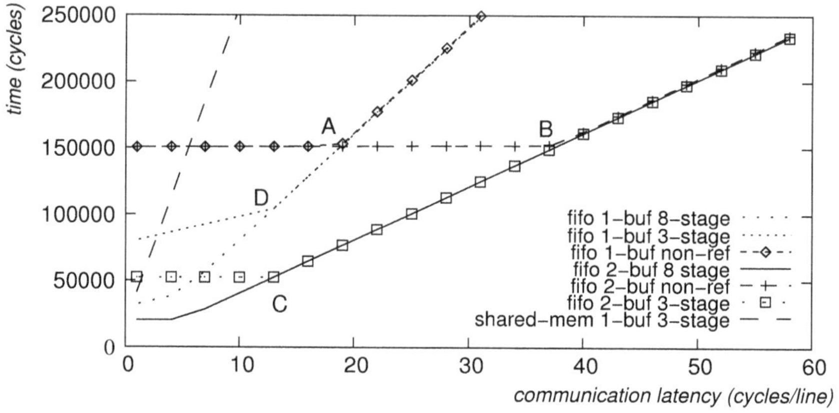

Figure 4.17: Performance results for the FIFO architecture.

non-refined models, we observe that they match each other until point A. After that point, as the communication latency increases, the single buffer model becomes communication bounded. The performance of the double buffer model is affected by the increased communication latency at point B, when the time to transfer a block of data becomes equal to the time it takes to perform an IDCT on a block of data. When we compare the refined models with the non-refined models, we observe that once the communication becomes a bottleneck (point A for single buffer and point B for double buffer), the advantage of having a pipelined execution unit disappears. When the models become communication bounded, the non-refined and refined models predict the same performance numbers. We note that a similar situation occurs at points C and D, when increased communication latencies negate the effect of having a longer pipeline. Finally, when we compare these results with the results of the shared memory architecture, we observe that in the latter, the performance is very quickly bounded by the communication, because increasing the communication latency causes contention on the shared bus. This makes the effect of pipelined execution very limited. For this reason, we only present the graph for the refined case with the 3-stage pipeline.

4.6 Conclusion

In this chapter, we have proposed and implemented a new mapping methodology for the Sesame co-simulation environment. The need for this new mapping methodology stems from the fact that refinement of architecture models in Sesame requires that the application events driving the architectural simulator should also be refined in order to match the architectural detail. Besides, such refinement should be supported in a way that allows for a smooth transition between different abstraction levels, without the need for reimplementing (parts) of the application model. Our methodology involves trace transformation and their implementations within the co-simulation framework via IDF dataflow models. Using examples and a simple experiment, we have shown that our method allows for effectively refining synchronization points as well as the granularity of data transfers and executions. We have also shown that, using IDF models, one could easily model different issues at the architecture level, such as task-level parallelism, intra-task parallelism, various communication policies, and pipeline execution stages inside a single processor. While doing all these, we kept the application model unaffected for maximum reusability.

5

Motion-JPEG encoder case studies

In the previous three chapters, we have dedicated each complete chapter to tackle and study a certain design issue, which we come across during different steps in the modeling and performance evaluation of an embedded system that is specified at the system-level. More specifically, in Chapter 2 we have seen the modeling and simulation methods and tools as they are provided by the Sesame environment. These include the application running engine PNRunner, Pearl discrete-event simulation language, and the YML structure description language.

Chapter 3 focussed on *design space pruning*, that is to reduce an exponential design space into a manageable size of points, which are superior with respect to some design criteria of choice. These choices, which occur during the mapping stage in Sesame, were mathematically modeled and subsequently solved using multiobjective optimizers taking into account three conflicting design criteria.

In Chapter 4, we next commenced on tackling problems such as *design space exploration* and *architectural model refinement*. In order to tackle the refinement issue systematically, we have identified application/architecture event traces, and subsequently defined trace transformations which model the aforementioned refinements. Moreover, we have incorporated dataflow actors into Sesame, which enabled us to realize the specified trace transformations within the co-simulation environment without altering the application model.

Chapters 3 and 4 were concluded with experiments, which have demonstrated the practical applicability and efficiency (in terms of design and evaluation time) of the proposed methods and tools for use in effective design space exploration.

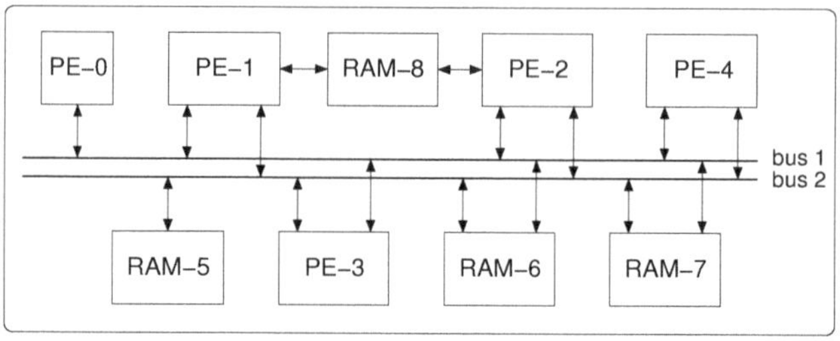

Figure 5.1: Metaplatform architecture model.

This chapter will put together all these methods and tools we have seen on a real design case study. More specifically, we take a designer systematically along the road from identifying candidate architectures, using analytical modeling and optimization (Chapter 3), to simulating these candidate architectures with our system-level simulation environment (Chapter 2). This simulation environment will subsequently allow for architectural exploration at different levels of abstraction (Chapter 4) while maintaining high-level and architecture independent application specifications. All these aspects are illustrated in the next section on an M-JPEG encoder application. What is more, in Section 5.2, we will show how system-level model calibration can be performed using additional tools from the Artemis workbench [79]. Eventually, using the same M-JPEG application, we will validate Sesame's performance estimations against real implementations on a prototyping hardware platform.

5.1 Sesame: Pruning, exploration, and refinement

In this case study, we demonstrate the capabilities of the Sesame environment which spans the *pruning*, *exploration*, and *refinement* stages in system-level design. More specifically, taking the Motion-JPEG (M-JPEG) encoder application, we demonstrate how Sesame allows a designer to systematically traverse the path from selecting candidate architectures by making use of analytical modeling and multiobjective optimization to simulating these candidate architectures with our system-level simulation environment. Subsequently, some selected architecture models are further refined and simulated at different levels of abstraction (facilitated by Sesame's dataflow-based refinement techniques) while still maintaining high-level and thus architecture-independent application models.

The application model of the M-JPEG encoder is already given by Figure 3.5 in Chapter 3. Figure 5.1 depicts the platform architecture under study, which consists of five processors and four memories connected by two shared buses and point-to-point links. Using our analytical modeling and multiobjective optimization techniques from Chapter 3, we intend to find promising instances of this platform architecture that lead to good mapping (in terms of performance, power, and cost criteria) of the M-JPEG encoder application. Subsequently, two of these candidate solutions will be further studied using system-level simulation.

Table 5.1: Parameters for processor and memory elements

Processor	Processing cap. (comp,comm)	Power cons. (comp,comm)	Cost
PE-0	(2x,2x)	(y,z)	k
PE-1	(5x,5x)	(4y,3z)	6k
PE-2	(3x,3x)	(3y,3z)	4k
PE-3	(3x,3x)	(3y,3z)	4k
PE-4	(3x,3x)	(3y,3z)	4k
Memory	Processing cap.	Power cons.	Cost
RAM-5	3x	5y	2k
RAM-{6-8}	x	2y	k

Table 5.1 provides the processor and memory characteristics which have been used during the multiobjective optimization process. In this design pruning phase, we have used relative processing capacities (x), power consumption during execution (y) and communication (z), and cost (k) values for each processor and memory in the platform architecture. We have used the MMPN problem module from PISA [12], which implements the analytical model introduced earlier in Chapter 3 of this thesis. The model, which was then implemented using GAlib [102], was first introduced in [35], and later re-implemented in PISA and further elaborated in [37] by making use of the multiobjective optimizers available from PISA. As we have seen in Chapter 3, the MMPN problem has mapping constraints which are defined by the allele sets. The allele set of a processor contains those application processes which can be mapped onto that processor. Table 5.2 shows the configuration used in our experiments. The constraint violations are handled by Algorithm 2 in Chapter 3.

The experiments reported here are obtained with the SPEA2 optimizer in PISA. Additional parameters for SPEA2 are as follows:

- population size = 100
- number of generations = $1,000$
- crossover probability = 0.8
- mutation probability = 0.5
- bit mutation probability = 0.01

Figure 5.2 presents the nondominated front as obtained by plotting 17 nondominated solutions which were found by SPEA2 in a single run. Before plotting, the objective function values were normalized with respect to the procedure explained in Section 3.3.4. The normalization procedure maps the objective function values into the $[0, 1]$ interval. This allows better visualization as objective functions scale independently. It took less than 30 secs. on a Pentium 4 machine at 2.8 GHz for SPEA2 to find all 17 nondominated solutions. However, search times can be dependent on factors such as the input size of the problem (i.e. number of application

Table 5.2: Processor characteristics

Processor	Allele set for the processor
PE-0	dct
PE-1	qc, dct, dmux, quant, rgb2yuv, vle, vid_in, vid_out
PE-2	qc, dct, dmux, quant, rgb2yuv, vle, vid_in, vid_out
PE-3	qc, dct, dmux, quant, rgb2yuv, vle, vid_in, vid_out
PE-4	qc, dct, dmux, quant, rgb2yuv, vle, vid_in, vid_out

processes, channels, architectural resources) and the amount of infeasibility (i.e. elements in the allele sets). The latter is due to constraints handling with a repair algorithm.

Table 5.3: Two solutions chosen for simulation.

Solution	Max processing time	Power cons.	Cost
sol 1	129338	1166	160
sol 2	193252	936	90

We have selected two nondominated solutions for further investigation by means of simulation. The objective functions values corresponding to these solutions are given in Table 5.3. The first solution *sol 1* is a faster implementation which uses three processing cores (PE-1, PE-2, PE-3), while *sol 2* uses only two processing cores (PE-0 and PE-1) and thus is more cost efficient. In both instances of the platform architecture, the processors are connected to a single common bus and communicate through shared memory (RAM-7). We modeled these two platform instances within Sesame, initially at a high abstraction level where the simulated architecture events are identical to the generated application events. Hence, the architecture model components are composed of nonrefined high-level processors and memory elements. The performance characteristics of the processors such as PE-0 and PE-1 are varied to reflect different types of processing cores that are present in the platform architecture. The resultant cycle counts from two system-level simulations for the target platform instances are tabulated in Table 5.4. Both system-level simulations involved an encoding of 11 frames with a resolution of 352x288 pixels. The simulations anticipate that *sol 1* will be a faster implementation than *sol 2*, which are in accord with the results of the analytical method in Table 5.3. Table 5.4 also gives the wall-clock time of the simulations on a Pentium 4 2.8 GHz machine, which is roughly 64 seconds for both cases. We should note that exact clock cycles may not be very accurate, as we have not done any calibration for tuning the parameters of the architecture model components. However, as we will show further in this chapter, more accurate results can be achieved by putting more modeling effort (such as putting more implementation details in the architecture model components by doing model refinement) and/or calibrating system-level models by getting feedback (e.g. exact number of execution cycles for certain operations) from lower-level simulations or prototype implementations

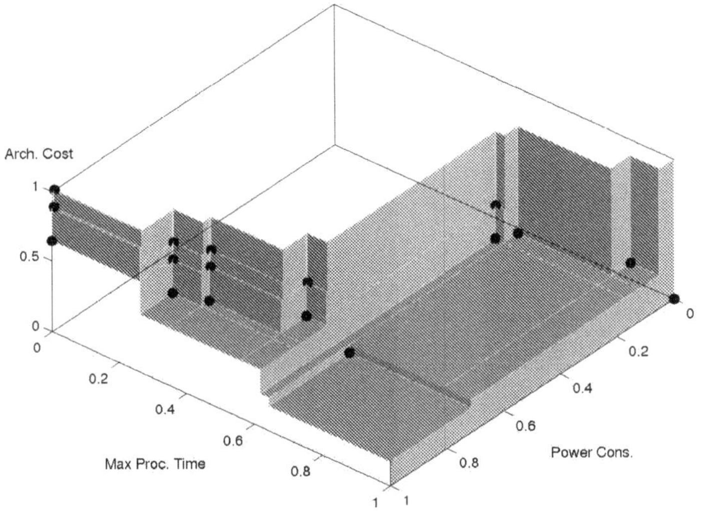

Figure 5.2: Nondominated front obtained by SPEA2.

on FPGA boards.

Table 5.4: Simulation of the two selected platform architectures.

Solution	Estimated cycle count	Wall-clock time (secs)
sol 1	40585833	≈64
sol 2	49816109	≈64

In the following experiments, we further focus on the DCT task in the M-JPEG application. This DCT application task operates on half (2:1:1) macroblocks which consist of two luminance (Y) blocks and two chrominance (U and V) blocks. Concerning the DCT task, we now would like to model more implementation details at the architecture level by making use of our IDF-based modeling techniques from Chapter 4. For this purpose, the first detail we add to the PE onto which the DCT task is mapped is an explicit preshift block which models the need to preshift luminance blocks, before a DCT is performed on them. Because the application DCT task will still generate course-grained DCT events, we need IDF models at the mapping layer which will transform (i.e. refine) the application event trace (from the DCT application task) into an architecture event trace which now must contain a preshift event. The required IDF graph for this trace transformation is given in Figure 5.3. When the IDF scheduler encounters four $R \rightarrow E \rightarrow W$ event sequences each referring to the processing of a single block inside a 2:1:1 half macroblock, it starts executing this graph by triggering the initial REPEAT-BEGIN actor by sending token(s) on its input. Subsequent firings of the IDF actors will generate preshift and 2D-DCT architecture-level events for the first two luminance blocks and only 2D-DCT events for the two following chrominance blocks. The gray ac-

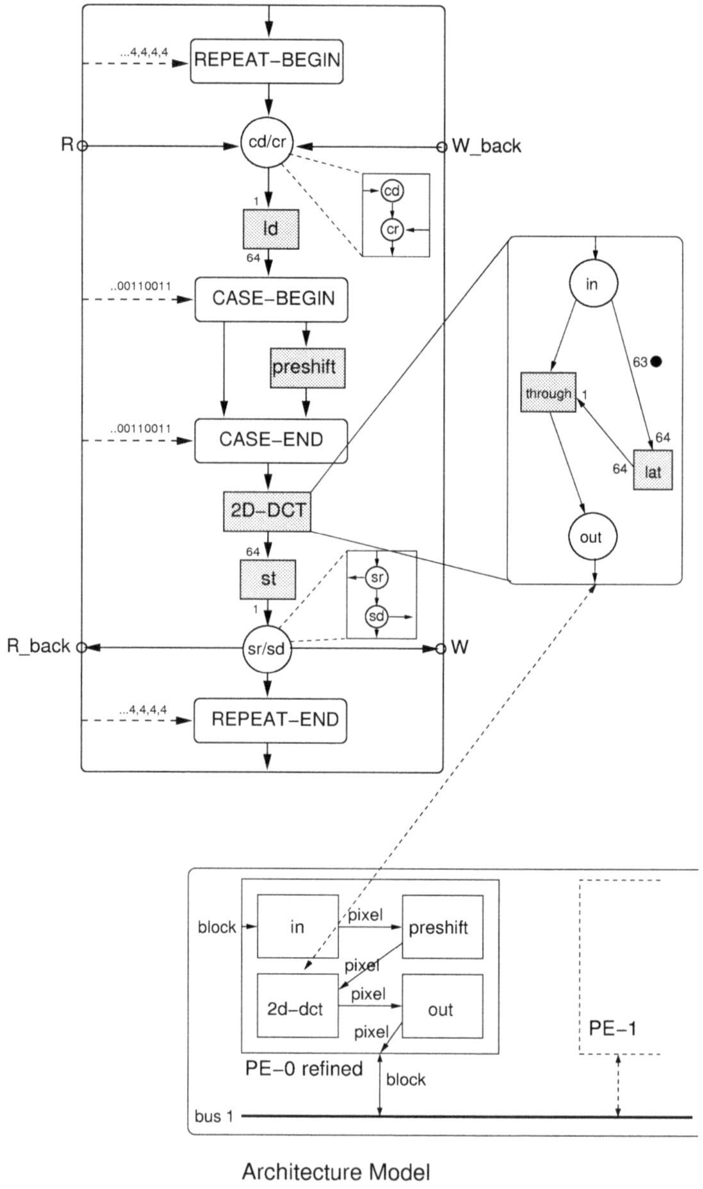

Figure 5.3: IDF graph refining the DCT task mapped on a processor without local memory.

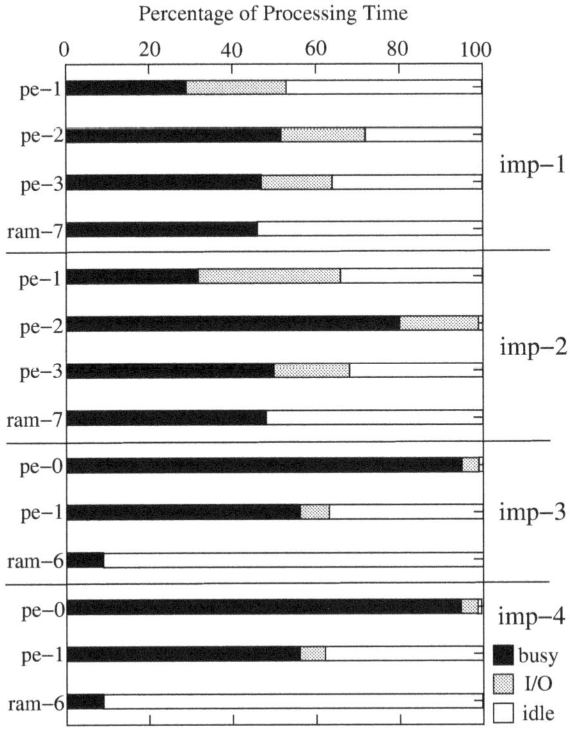

Figure 5.4: Simulation results showing the utilization of architecture components.

tors in Figure 5.3 are actually composite actors which perform a token exchange with the architecture model. The latter enables them to account for the latency of their action. The composite actors and the related token exchange mechanism were explained in Section 4.3.3 within the context of dataflow actors in Sesame.

The IDF graph also performs communication refinement by making the synchronizations explicit. In the previous chapter, we have modeled and studied such transformations that are applied on application event traces. Figure 5.3 shows the IDF graph for a PE without local memory. Because this PE cannot store data locally, it does an early `check-room` (*cr*) to allocate memory space to be able to write its output data immediately after computation. A PE with local memory could be modeled with a delayed *cr*, i.e. before the `store` (*st*) event in Figure 5.3.

In Table 5.5 we give the estimated performance results for both target architectures, simulated with and without local memory for the refined PE. The results suggest that having local memory to store computations improves the overall performance. The statistics in Figure 5.4 reveal that mapping the application tasks QC and DCT onto separate fast PEs (*sol 1*) results in a more balanced system. On the other hand, *sol 2* maps the computation intensive DCT task onto less powerful PE-0, which results in a cheaper implementation. However, the performance is limited by PE-0 in this case. Consequently, the memory used for communication is also

Table 5.5: Architecture refinement results - I

Imp.	Definition	Cycle count
imp-1	sol 1, PE-2 without local memory	43523731
imp-2	sol 1, PE-2 with local memory	41210599
imp-3	sol 2, PE-0 without local memory	47865333
imp-4	sol 2, PE-0 with local memory	47656269

underutilized. Because memory usage is limited in *sol 2*, adding local memory to PE-0 does not yield a significant improvement on performance.

Table 5.6: Architecture refinement results - II

Imp.	Definition	Cycle count
imp-5	sol 2, PE-0 without local memory, non-refined (black-box) DCT	29647393
imp-6	sol 2, PE-0 without local memory, refined (pipelined) DCT	29673684

The performance results for *sol 2* suggest to replace PE-0 with a faster application specific processing element (ASIP). The targeted PE-0 now has two pixel pipelines which make it possible to perform preshift and 2D-DCT operations in parallel. We have modeled the pipelined PE-0 in two distinct ways. The first model, which corresponds to implementation 5 in Table 5.6, is achieved by reducing the execution latencies associated with the preshift and 2D-DCT events in order to model a hardware implementation. These event latencies now approximate the pipelines to process a single pixel block. This is a quick way of modeling the effect of a pipelined processing element on the system.

Implementation 6 in Table 5.6, on the other hand, explicitly models the pipelines by refining the preshift and 2D-DCT operations at the architecture level. However, this is still done in a high-level fashion. The dataflow graph in the top right box in Figure 5.3 models the latency and throughput of the pipeline at the pixel level without actually modeling every single stage of the pipeline. We postpone further details concerning the abstract pipeline to the next section. The architecture-level events generated by the abstract pipeline IDF model are now mapped onto a refined architecture component which allows for parallel execution of preshift and 2D-DCT execute events. The simulation results in Table 5.6 reveal that performance estimations from both models are very close. This is normal because we neglect pipeline stalls in the abstract pipeline model. However, both models suggest a substantial increase in performance over implementation 3 in Table 5.5. As a next step, we could use a more detailed pipeline model that includes all pipeline stages as was done in Section 4.5 of the previous chapter.

With respect to wall-clock times, all simulations with the refined models in Table 5.5 and implementation 5 in Table 5.6 take around 65 seconds. Only implementation 6 in Table 5.6 takes 120 seconds due to the simulation of the DCT

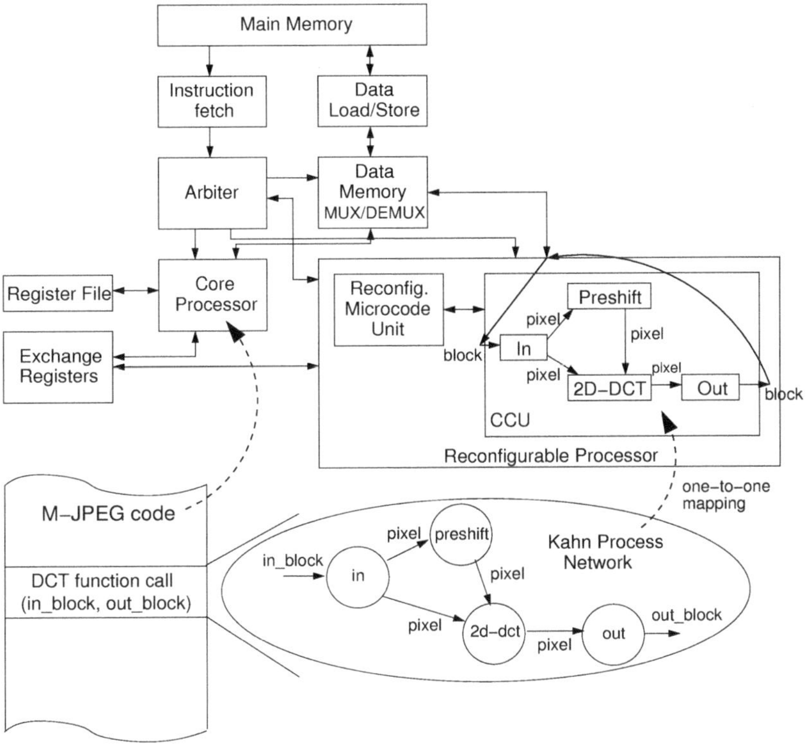

Figure 5.5: Calibration of the DCT task using the Compaan-Laura frameworks and the Molen platform architecture.

operation at the pixel level.

As a final remark, we should note that implementation 6 is actually a mixed-level simulation. This is due to the fact that PE-0 is refined to model (high-level) pipelines at the pixel level, while all other components in the system still operate at the level of entire pixel blocks. The latter is the granularity of the application events which drive the architectural simulation. Furthermore, the application model was kept intact during all these experiments which fosters its reuse.

5.2 Artemis: Calibration and validation

In this section, we report additional experiments with the M-JPEG encoder application in order to demonstrate how model calibration and validation can be performed using the Artemis workbench [79], which also includes our system-level modeling and exploration Sesame. Besides Sesame, Artemis workbench includes the Compaan-Laura tool sets and the Molen platform architecture. In Section 2.7, we have identified two calibration techniques which could be applied for calibrating system-level models for software and hardware target implementations. To calibrate programmable components (i.e. software implementation), we there proposed

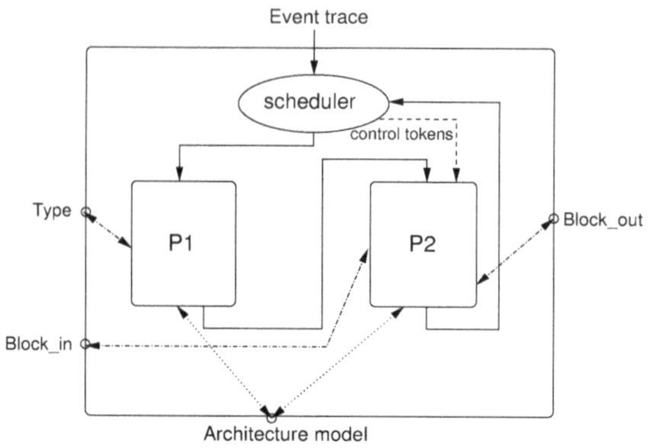

Figure 5.6: Virtual processor for DCT Kahn process.

coupling Sesame with low level (ISS/RTL level) microprocessor simulators. In the case of hardware implementations, we suggested using Compaan [57] for source code transformations, especially to obtain parallel application models (specified as Kahn process networks or KPNs) from sequential code, and the Laura tool [106] to generate synthesizable VHDL code (specific for an FPGA platform such as the Molen platform) for the given KPN input. The Molen platform [100], which is used for component calibration in Artemis, consists of a programmable processor and a reconfigurable unit and uses microcode to incorporate architectural support for the reconfigurable part. An overview of the Molen platform is given in Figure 5.5, where instructions are fetched from the main memory after which the arbiter partially decodes them to decide where they should be issued (to the core processor or the reconfigurable unit). Molen is realized in the Xilinx Virtex II Pro platform, which makes use of a PowerPC core for the core processor and the FPGA technology for the reconfigurable processor in Figure 5.5. We refer [76] for further details on the Artemis workbench.

For the experiment, we have selected the computationally intensive DCT task for calibration. This means using the technique from Section 2.7 for hardware implementations, the DCT task will be implemented in hardware in order to study its performance. The required steps in doing so are summarized in Figure 5.5. First, the code for the DCT task is isolated and used as an input to the Compaan tool set, which then generates a (parallel) KPN specification for the DCT task. As shown in Figure 5.5, this KPN consists of four tasks (`in`, `out`, `preshift`, and `2d-dct`) which communicate pixels over the internal Kahn channels. However, the `in` and `out` tasks read and write pixel blocks, as the rest of the M-JPEG application operates at the pixel block level. Using Laura, the KPN of the DCT task was translated into a VHDL implementation, where e.g. the `2d-dct` is realized as a 92-stage pipelined IP block that is mapped onto the reconfigurable processor (CCU) in the Molen platform. The rest of the M-JPEG application is mapped onto Molen's PowerPC processor. This allows us to study the hardware DCT implementation within the context of the M-JPEG application. The reason doing this was to calibrate the parameters of our system-level architecture models.

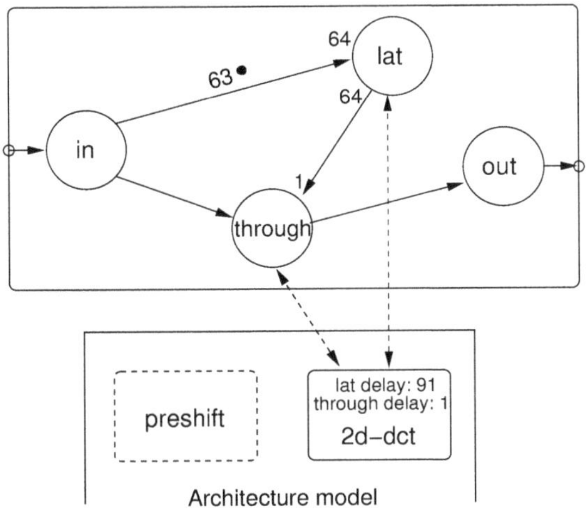

Figure 5.7: SDF graph for the 2D-DCT composite actor in Figure 5.3 which models an abstract pipeline.

For the validation of Sesame's performance estimations, we have modeled the Molen calibration platform in Sesame. This has given us the opportunity to compare high-level numbers from system-level simulation against the real numbers from the actual implementation. The resulting system-level Molen model contains Molen's PowerPC and CCU cores which are connected two-way using two unidirectional FIFO buffers. Following the mapping in Laura-to-Molen, we mapped the DCT process in the M-JPEG KPN application onto the CCU component while all other Kahn processes are mapped onto the PowerPC. The CCU in the system-level architecture model is also refined to model the pixel-level DCT implementation in Molen's CCU. However, the system-level PowerPC model component was not refined, implying that it operates at the pixel-block level which results in a mixed-level simulation. We should stress the fact that the M-JPEG application is again left intact during this experiment. This means that the refinement of the application events in order to drive the refined CCU component was once again realized using our dataflow-based refinement method.

The refined virtual processor of the DCT Kahn process at the mapping layer consists of several layers of hierarchy. The top level in hierarchy is depicted in Figure 5.6. The top-level IDF graph contains two composite actors P1 and P2 which refer to the two alternating patterns of application events that the DCT process generates. The pattern P1 results from the code (residing in the DCT process) that finds the location of the next half macro-block to be processed. Because we are not interested in this pattern, P1 is not further refined. On the other hand, P2 denotes the actual processing (reading pixel blocks, executing preshift and 2d-dct operations, and writing pixel blocks) of a half macro-block. The channels named *Type*, *Block_in*, and *Block_out* in Figure 5.6 refer to channels to/from the other virtual processors, while the dotted channels represent token exchange channels to/from the architecture model. The internal IDF graph for the composite P2 actor,

Table 5.7: Validation results of the M-JPEG experiment.

	Real Molen (cycles)	Sesame simulation (cycles)	Error (%)
Full SW implementation	84581250	85024000	0.5
DCT mapped onto CCU	39369970	40107869	1.9

in fact, corresponds to the same IDF graph that was used in implementation 6 for refining the DCT task. Hence, this IDF graph was already given (in the top left box in Figure 5.3) and explained in the previous section. A notable addition to the discussion there is that the 1-to-64 and 64-to-1 up- and down-samplings performed after the ld and st operations are for pixel-block to pixels and pixels to pixel-block conversions, respectively.

As previously mentioned, the `preshift` and `2d-dct` tasks are implemented as pipeline units in the Molen platform. Their corresponding system-level models are realized by incorporating SDF graphs into the composite preshift and 2D-DCT actors in Figure 5.3, which model the pipelined execution semantics with abstract pipelines. Figure 5.7 shows the abstract pipeline for the 2D-DCT actor. It simply models the latency and throughput of the pipeline while assuming that no bubbles can occur within the processing of the same pixel block. We should note that a more detailed pipeline model which includes pipeline stalls during execution could be built and used here as well. However, this would require extra modeling effort.

When we consider the SDF graph in Figure 5.7, for each pixel, the `in` actor fires a token to the `lat` and `through` actors. We observe that the channel between the `in` and `lat` actors contains 63 initial tokens, which means that after the first pixel from a pixel block, the `lat` actor will fire. The latter will produce a token exchange with the architecture model, where the latency of the `lat` actor is simulated for 91 cycles. Because the actual 2D-DCT component pipeline has 92 stages, 91 cycles of latency accounts for the first pixel from the pixel block to traverse through the pipeline until the last stage. Following this, the `through` will fire 64 times, each with a latency of 1 cycle, accounting for the 64 pixels leaving the pipeline one by one.

Throughout the validation experiments reported here, we have used low level information – pipeline depth of units, latencies for reading/writing/processing pixels, etc. – from the Compaan-Laura-Molen implementation to calibrate Sesame's system-level models. To check whether the calibrated system-level models produce accurate performance estimations, we compared the performance of the M-JPEG encoder application executed on the real Molen platform with the results from the Sesame framework. Table 5.7 shows the validation results obtained by running the same input sequences on both environments. The results in Table 5.7 include two cases in which all application tasks are performed in software (on the PowerPC) and in which the DCT task is realized in hardware (on the CCU). These results have been obtained without any tuning of the system-level models with Molen's execution results. The results show that Sesame's system-level performance estimations are relatively accurate, which in turn suggest that our dataflow-based architecture model refinement, which facilitates multi-level architectural exploration while keeping the application model intact, is highly promising.

5.3 Conclusion

This chapter has demonstrated most of the capabilities of the Sesame framework and the Artemis workbench which include, besides Sesame, the Compaan-Laura tool-sets and the Molen platform architecture. Using experiments with the M-JPEG encoder application, we showed how design space pruning and exploration, architectural refinement, model calibration and validation could be accomplished from the perspective of the Sesame-Artemis approach.

Future work on Sesame-Artemis may include i) extending application and architecture model component libraries with new components operating at multiple levels of abstraction, ii) further improving its accuracy with other techniques such as trace calibration [98], iii) performing further validation experiments to test accuracy improvements, and finally iv) applying Sesame-Artemis to other application domains.

6

Real-time issues

In this chapter, we will describe some recent work which has not yet been incorporated into the Sesame framework. The work performed here stems from the basic question that, using Sesame, whether one could model and evaluate embedded systems with some real-time constraints as well. The results obtained so far, which are to be reported here, have already established the necessary theoretical underpinnings of such an environment. However, more practical utilization of these results still remains as future work. The experiments reported at the end of this chapter were conducted on synthetic task systems which were taken from the literature. Although these experiments provide good evidence for the practical usefulness of our results, as already mentioned, we are still lacking an environment (ideally an extended Sesame framework), in which we can execute real-time application tasks, map these tasks onto platform architectures, and finally identify whether they complete their execution without missing any deadline.

In order to perform this, the code residing inside each Kahn process can be extended to a conditional real-time code by simply adding an additional deadline parameter to the application events which represent them. Hence, now an application event generated by an application model is not only associated with an execution requirement (which was the case until this chapter), but also with a deadline requirement, which states the length of the time interval in which the execution of this event should be completed.

In the next section, we start introducing important concepts, such as, for example, what we exactly mean by a conditional real-time code, and subsequently identify two important problems within the context of real-time code scheduling, which will be tackled throughout the rest of the chapter.

6.1 Problem definition

In general, real-time embedded systems are assumed to run infinitely on limited resources and the scheduling in this domain tries to address the problem of finding a set of rules to schedule independent tasks on these limited resources. There exists a trade-off between the generality of the task model (a measure of accuracy) and the analyzability of the system modeled. As a result of this, many task models have been proposed in the past which differ in terms of their expressive power and the complexity to analyze them. In general terms, a real-time system is a collection of independent tasks, each generating a sequence of subtasks associated with a ready-time, an execution requirement, and a deadline. Different task models may specify different constraints on these parameters. For example, the multiframe model [72] permits task cycling but ignores deadlines while the generalized multiframe [9] adds explicit deadlines to the multiframe model. Furthermore, the system may be composed of one or more processors and the task execution may be preemptive or non-preemptive. The schedulability analysis of such a real-time system is to identify whether it is possible to guarantee for each task a processor time equal to its execution requirement within the time duration between its ready-time and deadline.

For many embedded systems running on limited resources, preemptive scheduling may be very costly and the designers of such systems may prefer non-preemptive scheduling despite its relatively poor theoretical results. This is mainly due to the large runtime overhead incurred by the expensive context switching and the memory overhead due to the necessity of storing preempted task states. There is also a trade-off between static (tasks are given unique priorities offline) and dynamic scheduling (tasks are given priorities online) policies. While static scheduling has a very low CPU overhead, run-time scheduling may be necessary for better processor utilization.

Conditional real-time code. Embedded real-time processes are typically implemented as event-driven code blocks residing in an infinite loop. The first step in the schedulability analysis of such real-time code is to obtain an equivalent task model which reveals the control flow information. In the following conditional real-time code, execution requirement and deadline of subtasks v (representing code blocks) are shown with the parameters e and d, respectively. This means that whenever a subtask v is triggered by an external event, the code block corresponding to that subtask should be executed on the shared processing resources for e units of time within the next d units of time from its triggering time in order to satisfy its real-time constraints.

```
while (external_event)
    execute v1          /* with (e1, d1) */
    if (X) then         /* depends on system state */
        execute v2          /* with (e2, d2) */
    else
        execute v3          /* with (e3, d3) */
    end if
end while
```

The traditional analysis of such conditional codes, which depends on identifying the branch with the worst case behavior, does not work in this case. The branch with the worst case behavior depends on the system conditions that are external to the task. Consider the situation $(e_2 = 2, d_2 = 2)$ and $(e_3 = 4, d_3 = 5)$. If another subtask with $(e = 1, d = 1)$ is to be executed simultaneously, then the branch (e_2, d_2) is the worst case, whereas if the other subtask is with $(e = 2, d = 5)$, then the branch (e_3, d_3) corresponds to the worst case.

Previous results. There is a tremendous amount of work on scheduling even if we restrict ourselves to the uniprocessor case, history of which goes back at least to [68]. While some work in the real-time embedded systems domain tries to improve modeling accuracy, in one way or another generalizing the restrictions in [68] that has very desirable theoretical results, some other tries to answer schedule-theoretic questions arising in the generalized models. Most task models assume event-triggered independent tasks. However, there are also heterogeneous models considering mixed time/event-triggered systems [83] and systems with data and control dependencies [82]. The recurring real-time task model [7], on which we focus in this study, is a generalization of the previously introduced models, such as the recurring branching [6], generalized multiframe [9], multiframe [72] and sporadic [71] models. It can be shown that any of these task models corresponds to a special instance of the recurring task model, which in turn implies that it supersedes all previous models in terms of its expressive power. With respect to dynamic scheduling, it has been proved for both preemptive [68] and non-preemptive uniprocessor cases [19] that Earliest Deadline First (EDF) scheduling (among the ready tasks, a task with an earlier deadline is given a higher priority online) is *optimal*. The latter means that if a task is schedulable by any scheduling algorithm, then it is also schedulable under EDF. Hence, the online scheduling problem on uniprocessors is completely solved, we can always schedule using EDF. On the other hand, analysis of static priority scheduling yields two problems [8]:

- *Priority testing.* Given a hard real-time task system and a unique priority assignment to these tasks, can the system be scheduled by a static-priority scheduler such that all subtasks will always meet their deadlines?

- *Priority assignment.* Given a hard real-time task system, what is the unique priority assignment to these tasks (if one exists) which can be used by a static-priority run-time scheduler to schedule these tasks such that all subtasks will always meet their deadlines?

However, neither of these issues could have been solved within the context of the recurring real-time task model (for both preemptive and non-preemptive cases) up to this date and no optimal solution is known.

Our contributions. The priority assignment problem can be attacked by simply assigning a priority to each task in the system, and then checking if the assignment is feasible. However, for a system of n tasks, this approach has a complexity of $n!$ which grows too fast. Therefore, it does not provide a polynomial reduction from priority assignment to priority testing. In this chapter, we study static priority scheduling of recurring real-time tasks. We focus on the *non-preemptive uniproces-*

sor case and obtain schedule-theoretic results for this case. To this end, we derive a sufficient (albeit not necessary) condition for schedulability under static priority scheduling, and show that this condition can be efficiently tested *provided that task parameters have integral values*. In other words, a testing condition is derived for the general *priority testing problem*, and efficient algorithms with run-times that are pseudo-polynomial with respect to the problem input size are given for the *integer-valued* case. In addition, it is shown that these results are not too pessimistic, on the contrary, they exhibit practical value as they can be utilized within a search framework to solve the *priority assignment problem*. We demonstrate this with examples, where in each case, an optimal priority assignment for a given problem is obtained within reasonable time, by first detecting good candidates using simulated annealing and then by testing them with the pseudo-polynomial time algorithm developed for priority testing.

The rest of the chapter is organized as follows: next section formally introduces the recurring real-time task model. Section 6.3 presents the schedulability condition for static priority schedulers. State-of-the-art with respect to dynamic scheduling is summarized in Section 6.4. In Section 6.5, we present a simulated annealing based priority assignment search framework. Section 6.6 presents experimental results. Finally, concluding remarks are given in Section 6.7.

6.2 Recurring real-time task model

A recurring real-time task T is represented by a directed acyclic graph (DAG) and a period $P(T)$ with a unique source vertex with no incoming edges and a unique sink vertex with no outgoing edges. Each vertex of the task represents a subtask and is assigned with an execution requirement $e(v)$ and a deadline $d(v)$ of real numbers. Each directed edge in the task graph represents a possible control flow. Whenever vertex v is triggered, the subtask corresponding to it is generated with ready time equal to the triggering time, and it must be executed for $e(v)$ units of time within the next $d(v)$ units of time. In the non-preemptive case which we consider[1], once a vertex starts being executed, it can not be preempted. Hence, it is executed until its execution time is completed. Only once it is finished with execution, another vertex which has been triggered possibly from another task, can be scheduled for execution. In addition, each edge (u, v) of a task graph is assigned with a real number $p(u, v) \geq d(u)$ called inter-triggering separation which denotes the minimum amount of time which must elapse after the triggering of vertex u, before the vertex v can be triggered.

The execution semantics of a recurring real-time task state that initially the source vertex can be triggered at any time. When a vertex u is triggered, then the next vertex v can only be triggered if there is an edge (u, v) and after at least $p(u, v)$ units of time has passed since the vertex u is triggered. If the sink vertex of a task T is triggered, then the next vertex of T to be triggered is the source vertex. It can be triggered at any time after $P(T)$ units of time from its last triggering. If there are multiple edges from vertex u which represents a conditional branch, among the

[1]The scheduling in Sesame is also non-preemptive.

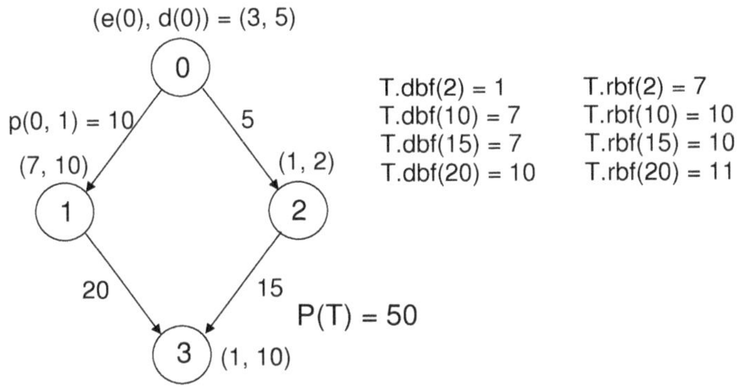

Figure 6.1: Computing the demand bound and request bound functions for T.

possible vertices only one vertex can be triggered. Therefore, a sequence of vertex triggerings $v_1, v_2, \cdots, v_k$ at time instants $t_1, t_2, \cdots t_k$ is legal if and only if there are directed edges (v_i, v_{i+1}) and $p(v_i, v_{i+1}) \leq t_{i+1} - t_i$ for $i = 1, \cdots, k$. The real-time constraints require that the execution of v_i should be completed during the time interval $[t_i, t_i + d(v)]$.

Schedulability analysis of a task system. A task system $\mathcal{T} = \{T_1, \cdots, T_k\}$ is a collection of task graphs, the vertices of which are triggered independently. A triggering sequence for such a task system $\mathcal{T}$ is legal if and only if for every task graph T_i, the subsequence formed by combining only the vertices belonging to T_i constitutes a legal triggering sequence for T_i. In other words, a legal triggering sequence for $\mathcal{T}$ is obtained by merging together (ordered by triggering times, with ties broken arbitrarily) legal triggering sequences of the constituting tasks. The schedulability analysis of a task system $\mathcal{T}$ deals with determining whether under all possible legal triggering sequences of $\mathcal{T}$, the subtasks corresponding to the vertices of the tasks can be scheduled such that all their deadlines are met. Particularly, we are interested in the non-preemptive uniprocessor case.

6.2.1 Demand bound and request bound functions

The results on schedulability analysis in most previous work [8], [9], [19] and also in this work are based on the abstraction of a task T by two functions which are defined as follows [8]:

The demand bound function $T.dbf(t)$ takes a non-negative real number $t \geq 0$ and returns the maximum cumulative execution requirement by the subtasks of T that have both their triggering times *and* deadlines within any time interval of duration t. In other words, demand bound function $T.dbf(t)$ of task T denotes the maximum execution time asked by the subtasks of T within any time interval of length t, *if it is to meet all its deadlines.*

Similarly, *the request bound function* $T.rbf(t)$ takes a non-negative real number $t \geq 0$ and returns the maximum cumulative execution requirement by the subtasks of T that have their triggering times within any time interval of duration t.

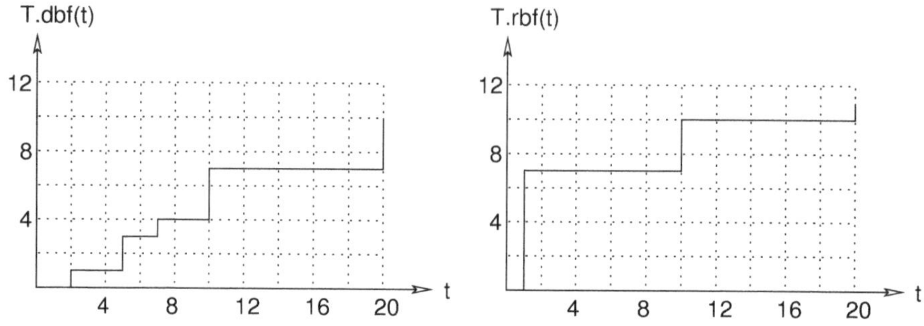

(a) Demand bound function $T.dbf(t)$.

(b) Request bound function $T.rbf(t)$.

Figure 6.2: The monotonically increasing functions $T.dbf(t)$ and $T.rbf(t)$ for the task T in Figure 6.1. Note that $T.dbf(t) \leq T.rbf(t)$ for all $t \geq 0$.

In other words, request bound function $T.rbf(t)$ of task T denotes the maximum execution time asked by the subtasks of T within any time interval of length t, *yet all of which is not necessarily to be completed within t.* From the point of view in [8], it can also be considered as the *maximum amount of time* for which T could deny the processor to tasks with lower priority over some interval of length t.

In Figure 6.1, we give an illustrative example. In this graph, $T.dbf(2) = 1$ as vertex v_2 can be triggered in the beginning of a time interval of length $t = 2$ and should be completed within this time interval in order to meet its deadline. Similarly, $T.dbf(20) = 10$ due to a possible triggering sequence of vertices v_0 and v_1 within any time interval of length $t = 20$.

In the same graph, $T.rbf(2) = 7$ because vertex v_1 can be triggered within 2 units of time. Similarly, $T.rbf(20) = 11$ due to a possible legal triggering sequence of v_3, v_0, v_1 at time instants $t_1 = 0$, $t_2 = 10$, $t_3 = 20$ within a time interval of $t = 20$. It can be shown by exhaustively enumerating all possible vertex triggerings of T that there exists no other sequence of vertex triggerings with a cumulative execution requirement that would exceed 11 within $t = 20$. Also notice that in the mentioned vertex triggering, the deadline requirements state that v_3 and v_0 should be completed by the time instants $t_1 + 10 = 10$ and $t_2 + 5 = 15$ which are both within t, while the deadline requirement for v_1 is at $t_3 + 10 = 30$ which is outside t. In Figure 6.2, we have plotted $T.dbf(t)$ and $T.rbf(t)$ functions values of the task T in Figure 6.1 for $t \leq 20$. It should be clear that both functions are monotonically increasing and $T.dbf(t) \leq T.rbf(t)$ holds for all $t \geq 0$.

We should note that the schedulability condition for static priority schedulers derived in Section 6.3 is solely based on $T.rbf(t)$. The reason for including $T.dbf(t)$ in our discussion is due to the fact that the schedulability conditions for dynamic priority schedulers [8], [19] are based on $T.dbf(t)$. As a consequence we need $T.dbf(t)$ in Section 6.4, where we summarize some earlier results for dynamic priority schedulers. The latter is done for the purpose of giving the whole state-of-

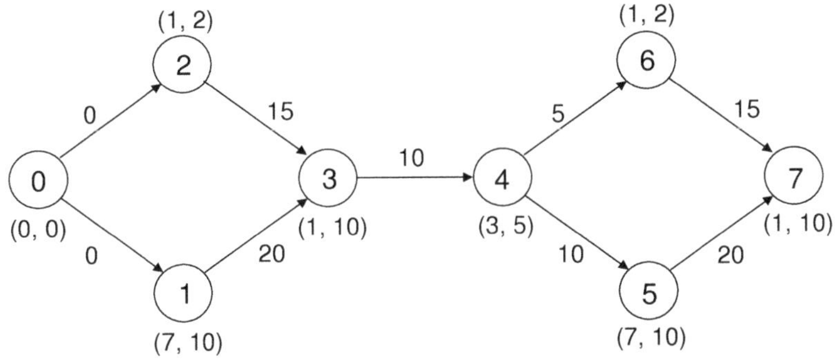

Figure 6.3: Transformed task graph T' for T in Figure 6.1.

the-art in non-preemptive scheduling within the context of the recurring real-time task model. In the following section we provide an efficient algorithm for computing $T.rbf(t)$. Similar techniques also yield an efficient algorithm for computing $T.dbf(t)$ and can be found in [19]. What is more, if some error can be tolerated, heuristics with better run-times can also be used in practice to estimate both demand bound and request bound functions values. However, the latter is out of the scope of this chapter and the interested reader is directed to [18].

6.2.2 Computing request bound function

First we are going to compute $T.rbf(t)$ for small values of t in which the source vertex is either not triggered, or is triggered only once. Then using results of [8], we will provide an expression for any t. In this way, the effect of recurring behavior of the task model can be included in the calculations.

Computing $T.rbf(t)$ for small t. To obtain all vertex triggerings, in which the source vertex is either not triggered or is triggered only once, we take two copies of the original DAG, add an edge from the sink vertex of the first copy to the source vertex of the second copy (by setting the inter-triggering separation equal to the deadline of the sink vertex of the first copy), and then delete the source vertex of the first copy. To make the resulting graph a DAG, we add a dummy source vertex to the first copy with $(e, v) = (0, 0)$. Starting from a transformed task graph which is not a DAG, [8] enumerates all paths in the task graph to compute $T.rbf(t)$ which has an exponential complexity while [19] starts from T and neglects the recurring behavior. Based on dynamic programming, we now give an incremental pseudo-polynomial time algorithm[2] to compute $T.rbf(t)$ for tasks with integral execution requirements and inter-triggering separations[3]. Let there be n vertices in T', $v_0, \cdots, v_{n-1}$. As shown in Figure 6.3, the vertex indices of T' are assigned

[2]A pseudo-polynomial time algorithm for an integer-valued problem is an algorithm whose running time is polynomial in the input size and in the values of the input integers. See [51] for a nice coverage.

[3]Computing $T.rbf(t)$ remains NP-hard even if the parameters (i.e. execution requirements, deadlines and inter-triggering separations) of the recurring real-time task model are restricted to integer numbers [20].

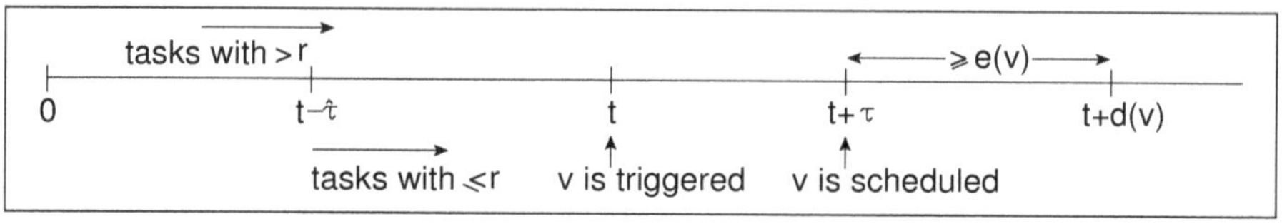

Figure 6.4: Scheduling scenario in Theorem 1.

such that there can be an edge from v_i to v_j only if $i < j$. Let $t_{i,e}$ be the *minimum time interval* within which the task T can have an execution requirement of *exactly* e time units due to some legal triggering sequence, considering only a subset of vertices from the set $\{v_0, \cdots, v_i\}$. Similarly, let $t^i_{i,e}$ be the *minimum time interval* within which a sequence of vertices from the set $\{v_0, \cdots, v_i\}$ and *ending* with vertex v_i, can have an execution of *exactly* e time units. Apparently, $E_{max} = (n-1)e_{max}$ where $e_{max} = \max\{e(v_i), i = 1, \cdots, n-1\}$ is an upperbound for $T.rbf(t)$ for any small $t \geq 0$.

Algorithm 3 computes $T.rbf(t)$ for small t in pseudo-polynomial time for tasks with integral $e(v) \geq 0$. Starting from the sequence $\{v_0\}$ and adding one vertex to this set in each iteration, the algorithm builds an array of minimal time intervals ending at the last vertex added for all execution requirement values between 0 and E_{max}, i.e. it computes $t^i_{i,e}$. Then using this result and the result of the previous calculation ($t_{i-1,e}$), it computes $t_{i,e}$ by taking their minimum. Once all vertices are processed and an array of minimal time intervals is built, the algorithm makes a lookup in the array and returns the maximum execution requirement for a given small t. It has a running time of $O(n^3 E_{max})$.

Computing $T.rbf(t)$ for any t. Once $T.rbf(t)$ is known for small t, the following expression from [8] can be used to calculate it for any t.

$$T.rbf(t) = \max\{(\lfloor t/P(T)\rfloor - 1)E(T) + T.rbf(P(T) + t \bmod P(T)), \lfloor t/P(T)\rfloor E(T) + T.rbf(t \bmod P(T))\}, \quad (6.1)$$

where $E(T)$ denotes maximum possible cumulative execution requirement on any path from the source to the sink vertex of T.

6.3 Schedulability under static priority scheduling

In this section, we derive a sufficient condition for schedulability under static priority scheduling. It is based on the abstraction of a recurring real-time task in terms of its request bound function.

Theorem 1 *(Erbas et al. [36], [34]) Given a task system $\mathcal{T} = \{T_1, \cdots, T_k\}$, where the task T_r has priority r, $0 \leq r \leq k$, and $r < q$ indicates that T_r has a higher priority than T_q. The task system is static priority schedulable if for all tasks T_r the following condition holds: for any vertex v of any task T_r, $\exists \tau$ with*

Algorithm 3 Computing $T.rbf(t)$ for small t

Require: Transformed task graph T', a real number $t \geq 0$
Ensure: $T.rbf(t)$

for $e = 0$ to E_{max} **do**

$$t_{0,e} \leftarrow \begin{cases} 0 & \text{if } e(v_0) \geq e \\ \infty & \text{otherwise} \end{cases}$$

$t^0_{0,e} \leftarrow t_{0,e}$
end for
for $i = 0$ to $n-2$ **do**
for $e = 0$ to E_{max} **do**
Assume there are directed edges from the vertices $v_{i_1}, v_{i_2}, \cdots, v_{i_k}$ to v_{i+1}

$$t^{i+1}_{i+1,e} \leftarrow \begin{cases} \min\{t^{i_j}_{i_j, e-e(v_{i+1})} + p(v_{i_j}, v_{i+1}) \\ \text{such that } j = 1, \cdots, k\} & \text{if } e(v_{i+1}) < e \\ 0 & \text{if } e(v_{i+1}) \geq e \end{cases}$$

$t_{i+1,e} \leftarrow \min\{t_{i,e}, t^{i+1}_{i+1,e}\}$
end for
end for
$T.rbf(t) \leftarrow \max\{e \mid t_{n-1,e} \leq t\}$

$0 \leq \tau \leq d(v) - e(v)$ *for which*

$$e^{>r}_{max} + T_r.rbf(t - p^{T_r}_{min}) + \sum_{i=1}^{r-1} T_i.rbf(t+\tau) \leq t + \tau, \qquad \forall t \geq 0 \quad (6.2)$$

where $e^{>r}_{max} = \max\{e(v') \mid v' \textit{is a vertex of } T_j, j = r+1, \cdots, k\}$ *and* $p^{T_r}_{min} = \min\{p(u, u') \mid u \textit{ and } u' \textit{ are vertices of } T_r\}$.

Proof: Let v be any vertex of the task T_r with an execution requirement $e(v)$ and a deadline $d(v)$. Consider the following scenario which is also depicted in Figure 6.4:

Let v be triggered at time t and be scheduled at time $t + \tau$. We assume that $t - \hat{\tau}$ is the first time before time t where the processor has no task with priority $\leq r$ to execute. Hence, at this time the processor is either idle or executing a task with priority $> r$. On the other hand, $t - \hat{\tau}$ is also the time where at least one vertex of a task graph with priority $\leq r$ was triggered. Under these conditions, the *upperbound* for the total remaining execution requirement before the vertex v can be scheduled at time $t + \tau$ is composed of

- the remaining execution requirement of some task triggered before time $t - \hat{\tau}$: $e^{>r}_{max}$,
- the execution requirement of the task T_r (not including v) during time interval $[t - \hat{\tau}, t]$: $T_r.rbf(\hat{\tau} - p^{T_r}_{min})$ where $p^{T_r}_{min}$ is the minimal inter-triggering separation in T_r,

Algorithm 4 Schedulability under static priority scheduling

Require: Task system $T_r \in \mathcal{T}$ with unique r
Ensure: $decision$
  $decision \leftarrow yes$
  for all $T_r \in \mathcal{T}$ and **for all** $v \in T_r$ and **for all** $t \geq 0$ **do**
    $flag \leftarrow 0$
    $e_{max}^{>r} \leftarrow \max\{e(v') \mid v' \in T_i, i > r)\}$
    $p_{min}^{T_r} \leftarrow \min\{p(u, u') \mid u, u' \in T_r)\}$
    $\mathcal{T}_{<r} \leftarrow \mathcal{T} \backslash \{T_i \mid i \geq r\}$
    $\tau_{max} \leftarrow d(v) - e(v)$
    for $\tau = 0$ to τ_{max} **do**
      if $e_{max}^{>r} + T_r.rbf(t - p_{min}^{T_r}) + \sum_{T \in \mathcal{T}_{<r}} T.rbf(t + \tau) \leq t + \tau$ **then**
        $flag \leftarrow 1$
      end if
    end for
    if $flag = 0$ **then**
      $decision \leftarrow no$
    end if
  end for
  return $decision$

- the total execution requirement of the tasks with priority $< r$ during time interval $[t - \hat{\tau}, t + \tau]$: $\sum_{i=1}^{r-1} T_i.rbf(\tau + \hat{\tau})$.

Therefore, within $[t - \hat{\tau}, t + \tau]$, the upperbound for the total execution requirement is

$$e_{max}^{>r} + T_r.rbf(\hat{\tau} - p_{min}^{T_r}) + \sum_{i=1}^{r-1} T_i.rbf(\tau + \hat{\tau}). \tag{6.3}$$

We define $I[t - \hat{\tau}, t + \tau]$ to be the processor idle time during time interval $[t - \hat{\tau}, t + \tau]$. If we show that the *lowerbound* for $I[t - \hat{\tau}, t + \tau]$ is non-negative, then we can conclude that the task system is schedulable. The lowerbound for $I[t - \hat{\tau}, t + \tau]$ can be written as,

$$(t + \tau) - (t - \hat{\tau}) - (e_{max}^{>r} + T_r.rbf(\hat{\tau} - p_{min}^{T_r}) + \sum_{i=1}^{r-1} T_i.rbf(\tau + \hat{\tau})). \tag{6.4}$$

By the condition (6.2) in Theorem 1, (6.3) is bounded by $\tau + \hat{\tau}$. Substituting this in (6.4), we obtain,

$$I[t - \hat{\tau}, t + \tau] \geq 0. \tag{6.5}$$

Hence, all tasks scheduled before vertex v meet their deadlines at $t + \tau$. The condition $0 \leq \tau \leq d(v) - e(v)$ ensures that v also meets its deadline. ■

Theorem 1 can be used to construct Algorithm 4 which solves the *priority testing problem* as defined in Section 6.1. Algorithm 4 simply checks if condition (6.2) holds for every vertex in the task system, and relies on Algorithm 3 and (6.1) for $T.rbf(t)$ calculations. Algorithm 4 along with Algorithm 3 is again a pseudo-polynomial time algorithm, since all other steps in Algorithm 4 can also be performed in pseudo-polynomial time. To see this, given any $T_r \in \mathcal{T}$, let $t^{T_r}_{max}$ denote the maximum amount of time elapsed among all vertex triggerings starting from the source and ending at the sink vertex, if every vertex of T_r is triggered at the earliest possible time without violating inter-triggering separations. Clearly, it is sufficient to test condition (6.2) in Algorithm 4 for $t_{max} = \max\{t^{T_r}_{max}, T_r \in \mathcal{T}\}$ times, which is pseudo-polynomially bounded. Therefore, Algorithm 4 is also a pseudo-polynomial time algorithm.

6.4 Dynamic priority scheduling

In this section we briefly summarize the state-of-the-art with respect to dynamic priority scheduling. Although our main focus in this chapter is on static priority scheduling, this section includes some results on dynamic priority scheduling that are either very generic (i.e. apply to many task models) or too important to exclude. Furthermore, we also think that it will make the overall discussion on scheduling more complete and provide the reader with a better understanding of the complete picture.

Among the dynamic scheduling policies, the Earliest Deadline First (EDF) scheduling algorithm, which schedules the subtask with the earliest deadline among all triggered subtasks at any time instant, is known to be optimal if preemptions are allowed [68]. In the non-preemptive case, EDF is optimal for independently executing tasks if the scheduler is work conserving or non-idle (i.e. if a subtask is triggered, then it has to be scheduled if the processor is idle). Both assumptions are quite general and apply to many task models such as sporadic, multiframe, generalized multiframe and recurring real-time task models.

Now we briefly summarize the schedulability condition for the recurring real-time task model with respect to non-preemptive EDF schedulers. Note that the definition of the $T.dbf^v(t)$ function used in the following theorem is identical to that of $T.dbf(t)$ with one additional constraint that the triggering sequence should end at the vertex v.

Theorem 2 *(Chakraborty et al. [19]) Given a task system $\mathcal{T} = \{T_1, \cdots, T_k\}$, where the task T_r has priority r, $0 \leq r \leq k$, and $r < q$ indicates that T_r has a higher priority than T_q. The task system is schedulable under EDF if and only if for all tasks T_r the following condition holds: for any vertex v of any task T_r,*

$$T_r.dbf^v(t + d(v)) + \sum_{i=1}^{r-1} T_i.dbf(t + d(v)) + e_{max} \leq t + d(v), \quad \forall t \geq 0 \qquad (6.6)$$

where e_{max} is the remaining execution requirement of the vertex that is in execution at time t.

Unlike the recurring real-time the task model, the task model in [19] has no periodic behavior. However, except the latter, it is the same task model. This has

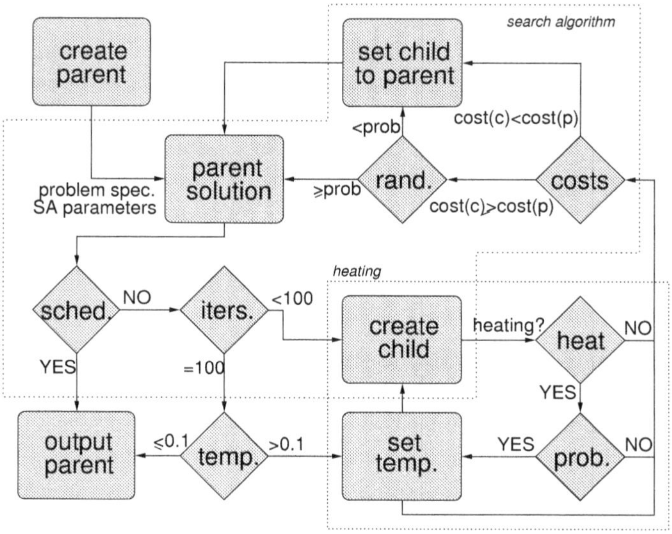

Figure 6.5: Overview of the simulated annealing (SA) framework. The *heating* is done only for the first 10 iterations in order to setup a reasonable initial temperature.

an effect on $T.dbf(t)$ and $T.dbf^v(t)$ values, but not on the condition (6.6). So, the condition still holds for the recurring real-time task model. Further details on Theorem 2, e.g. on the calculation of e_{max}, can be found in [19].

6.5 Simulated annealing framework

Simulated annealing (SA) can be viewed as a local search equipped with a random decision mechanism to escape from local optima. It is inspired by the annealing process in condensed matter physics. In this process, a matter is first melted and then slowly cooled in order to obtain the perfect crystal structure. In high temperatures, all the particles move randomly to high energy states. But as the temperature is decreased, the probability of such movements is also decreased.

In combinatorial optimization, the energy of a state corresponds to the cost function value of a feasible point and the temperature becomes a control parameter. We start with an arbitrary initial point and search its neighborhood randomly. If a better solution is found, then it becomes the current solution and the search continues from that point. But if it is a worse solution, then it may still be accepted with some probability depending on the difference in cost function values and the current temperature. Initially at high temperatures, the probability of accepting a worse solution is higher. The acceptance probability decreases, as the temperature is lowered. As a consequence, SA behaves like a random walk during early iterations, while it imitates hill climbing in low temperatures.

One of the strong features of SA is that it can find high quality solutions independent of the initial solution. In general, weak assumptions about the neighbor-

Table 6.1: Task system specifications.

$\mathcal{T}$	#ver./ed. in $\mathcal{T}$	#ver./ed. in $\mathcal{T}'$	$P(\mathcal{T})$	TS1	TS2	TS3	TS4	TS5	TS6	TS7
hou_c1	4/3	9/10	300	o	o	o	o	o	o	o
hou_c2	4/4	8/9	200	o	o	o	o	o	o	o
hou_c3	3/2	7/8	200	o	o	o	o	o	o	o
hou_c4	3/2	6/5	200	o	o	o	o	o	o	o
yen1	5/4	11/12	300	o	o	o	o	o	o	o
yen2	4/3	9/10	300	o	o	o	o	o	o	o
yen3	6/5	14/18	400	-	o	o	o	o	o	o
dick	5/5	11/14	400	-	-	o	o	o	o	o
hou_u1	10/13	21/30	700	-	-	-	o	o	o	o
hou_u2	10/16	20/33	500	-	-	-	-	o	o	o
hou_u3	10/15	22/41	600	-	-	-	-	-	o	o
hou_u4	10/14	22/36	700	-	-	-	-	-	-	o

hood and cooling scheme are enough to ensure convergence to optimal solutions. The key parameters in SA are temperature reduction rate and neighborhood definition. In most cases, it may require a lot of trials to adjust these parameters to a specific problem. We discuss the latter within the context of the schedulability problem in the next section. In order to utilize SA, we first formulate schedulability under static priority scheduling as a combinatorial optimization problem.

Problem formulation. Assume that we are given an instance (F, c) of an optimization problem, where F is the feasible set and c is the cost function. In our case F is the set of all possible priority assignments to tasks in $\mathcal{T}$ and c is the cost of such an assignment. Given a priority assignment f to tasks in $\mathcal{T}$, let *cond* represent the schedulability condition in (6.2), i.e. $cond = e_{max}^{>r} + T_r.rbf(t - p_{min}^{T_r}) + \sum_{T \in \mathcal{T}_{<r}} T.rbf(t + \tau)$. In this assignment, we define the cost of assigning priority r to a task, $c(T_r, t)$ as

$$c(T_r, t) = \begin{cases} 0 & \text{if } t = 0^- \\ c(T_r, t-1) & \text{if } \forall v \in T_r, \exists \tau \text{ s.t. } cond \leq t + \tau \\ |A| + c(T_r, t-1) & \text{if for some } v \in A \subseteq T_r, \nexists \tau \text{ s.t. } cond \leq t + \tau \end{cases}$$

where $0 \leq \tau \leq d(v) - e(v)$ and $0 \leq t \leq t_{max}^{T_r}$. Following this definition, the cost of a particular priority assignment to a task system becomes $c(f, \mathcal{T}) = \sum_{T_i \in \mathcal{T}} c(T_r, t_{max}^{T_r})$. The aim is to find the priority assignment $f \in F$ which minimizes $c(f, \mathcal{T})$.

Corollary 1 *A task system $\mathcal{T}$ is schedulable under static priority scheduling if $\exists f$ such that $c(f, \mathcal{T}) = 0$.*

Proof: The proof follows from the definition of $c(f, \mathcal{T})$. Clearly, for each task in $\mathcal{T}$, a violation of schedulability condition given by (6.2) increments the value of $c(f, \mathcal{T})$ by one. Hence a value of zero indicates that the schedulability condition is not violated. ∎

Table 6.2: Experimental results.

$\mathcal{T}$	$\#\mathcal{T}$	$t_{min}, t_{mid}, t_{max}$	sol. density	ES (secs.) ES1	ES2	search	SA (secs.) test	total
TS1	6	$10, 100, 189$	2.5%	$4,511$	333	22.15	6.25	28.40
TS2	7	$10, 100, 188$	2.14%	-	$2,856$	32.75	7.90	40.65
TS3	8	$10, 100, 184$	0.89%	-	$23,419$	64.40	9.30	73.70
TS4	9	$10, 100, 428$	-	-	-	88.60	37.80	126.40
TS5	10	$10, 100, 429$	-	-	-	170.75	53.40	224.15
TS6	11	$10, 100, 427$	-	-	-	311.05	62.80	373.85
TS7	12	$10, 100, 430$	-	-	-	331.45	86.45	417.90

6.6 Experimental results

In the previous section, we have introduced general characteristics of a simulated annealing framework. We now continue discussing those parameters of SA that are fine tuned according to the problem in hand. These parameters are used in all the experiments reported here. Figure 6.5 provides an overview of our framework. At first we use a heating mechanism to set the initial temperature. To do so, we start with $temp = 100$ and look at the first 10 iterations. If it is found that $prob(p \rightarrow s) < 0.5$ in one of these early iterations, then the temperature is increased such that the new solution is always accepted, i.e. current temperature is increased with $temp = |c(p, \mathcal{T}) - c(s, \mathcal{T})| / \ln(0.5)$ on that iteration. Remember that we are given an instance of the scheduling problem defined in the form (F, c) (see Section 6.5), and at each iteration, we search a neighborhood $N : F \rightarrow 2^F$ randomly at some feasible point $p \in F$ for an improvement. If such an improvement occurs at $s \in N(p)$ then the next point becomes s. But if $c(s, \mathcal{T}) > c(p, \mathcal{T})$ then s is still taken with a probability $prob(p \rightarrow s) = e^{-(c(s,\mathcal{T})-c(p,\mathcal{T}))/temp}$. In our experiments, the number of such iterations at each temperature is set to 100. The control parameter $temp$ is gradually decreased in accordance with a pre-defined cooling scheme. For the latter, we use a static reduction function $temp = 0.9temp$. Finally, we stop the search either when a feasible schedule is found or when the temperature drops under a certain value ($temp = 0.1$).

To illustrate the practical usefulness of our results, we have taken task examples from the literature and constructed new task systems using their different combinations. The first column in Table 6.1 refers to tasks used; tasks starting with hou_c and hou_u are Hou's clustered and unclustered tasks [50], respectively. Tasks starting with yen are Yen's examples on p.83 in [105]. Task dick is from [31]. These tasks were originally defined in different task models and do not possess all characteristics of a recurring real-time task. Topologically, some tasks have multiple source and/or sink vertices. In such cases, we have added dummy vertices (with null execution requirements) when necessary. In most cases, originally a deadline for each task was defined, contrary to recurring real-time task model in which a deadline is defined for each vertex (subtask). Therefore, we have defined deadlines for all vertices in all tasks (same in all task sets) using a random generator. Then in all task systems, we have tried to give maximal execution requirements to vertices in order to minimize the number of feasible priority assignments. We have

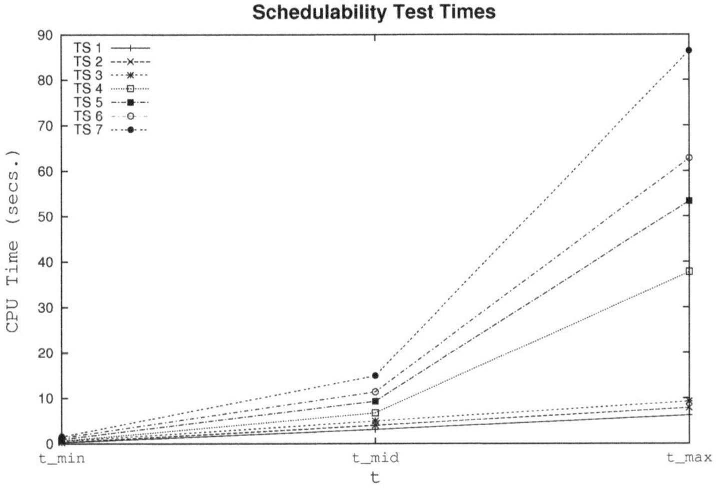

Figure 6.6: Schedulability test times. The advantage of using a combination of t_{min} and t_{mid} instead of t_{max} is clear from high computation times needed for t_{max}, especially for larger task systems TS 4, TS 5, TS 6 and TS 7.

achieved this by gradually increasing execution requirements until a small increase yielded an unschedulable task system.

In Appendix B, Figure B.1 and Table B.1 provide original task graphs and values of task parameters in our experiments, respectively. What is more, the details of transforming task graphs with multiple source and/or sink vertices are explained on illustrative examples given in Figure B.2. We provide a summary of most important parameters in columns 2, 3 and 4 of Table 6.1. The former two columns give the number of vertices and edges in task and transformed task graphs, while the latter provides task periods. As already stated, run-times of Algorithms 1 and 2 are pseudo-polynomially bounded with task sizes. The rest of the columns in Table 6.1 give task system specifications.

For numerical results, we have integrated Algorithms 1 and 2 as C functions into the introduced SA framework which was also implemented in C. The experiments reported here have been performed on a Pentium 3 PC with 600 MHz CPU and 320 MB RAM running Linux OS. For each task system scenario, we have performed 20 runs (with seeds from 1 to 20 for the random generator) searching for feasible schedules using the SA framework. All results given in Table 6.2 are arithmetic means of 20 runs. During the experiments, we observed that the schedulability condition is more sensitive to small values of t, and in most cases, it is enough to test up to the first t_{min} times to find a majority of non-optimal solutions. Therefore, in order to decrease search run-times by means of spending less time on non-optimal solutions, we have used a combination of t_{min} and t_{mid} values instead of the actual value t_{max}. In most cases, it was enough to test for the first t_{min} times to find a majority of non-optimal solutions. In the search, if a feasible solution for t_{min} was found, it was further tested for times up to t_{mid}. Only if the solution also passed

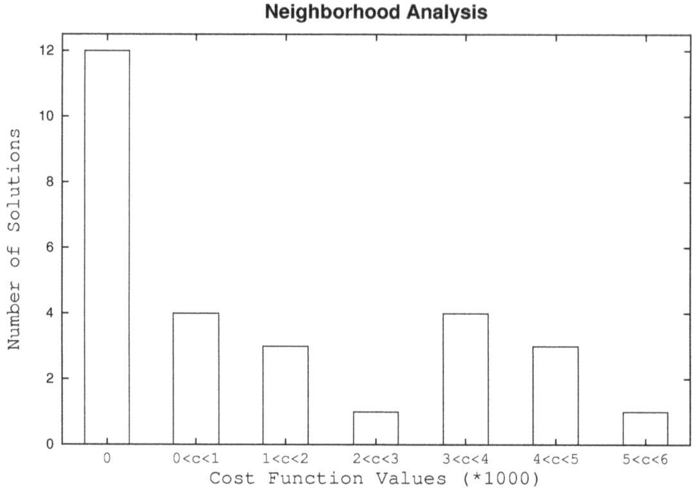

Figure 6.7: Neighborhood analysis. The distance from an optimal point and the value of the cost function are not strongly correlated.

this second test, it was output as a candidate for an optimal solution and the search was stopped. We call this CPU time spent on search as *SA search* and report their averages in column 7 of Table 6.2. Since SA tests many non-optimal solutions until it reaches an optimal one, using t_{min} instead of t_{max} at each iteration dramatically decreased run-times. In Figure 6.6, we plotted CPU times of schedulabilility tests with t_{min}, t_{mid} and t_{max} in all task system scenarios. If we compare CPU times of t_{min} and t_{max}, the difference lies between 15 to 25 times for TS1, TS2 and TS3, while for relatively larger task systems TS4, TS5, TS6 and TS7, it is between 45 to 60 times. Finally, all candidate solutions found have been tested once with t_{max}. We call the CPU time spent on this last step as *SA test*, and similarly report their averages in column 8 of Table 6.2. If a candidate solution fails in the last step, SA is started again and the next solution found is taken as the new candidate. However, it is interesting to note here that in our experiments, all first candidate solutions passed the last test, and therefore none of the SA search or test steps were repeated.

We have also performed exhaustive searches (ES) in cases where the size of task systems permitted to do so. The main reason behind this was to find out solution density, i.e. the number of optimal solutions in the feasible set. As a result of ES runs (given in column 4 in Table 6.2), we found out that solution densities in TS1, TS2 and TS3 scenarios are less than or equal to 2.5%. Two exhaustive searches ES1 and ES2 are given in columns 5 and 6 of Table 6.2. In ES1, all points in the feasible set were tested with t_{max} which took $4,511$ secs. for TS1. In ES2, we first tested all points with t_{min}, then only tested those points which passed the first test with t_{max}. Using this method, ES CPU time for TS1 decreased from $4,511$ to 333 secs. and we could also perform ES runs for TS2 and TS3.

Finally, we have taken one optimal solution for TS3 and examined all its 28 neighbors. The costs of these points are plotted in Figure 6.7. Despite a significant number of other optimal solutions around this solution, there are also some points with moderate to very high costs. This shows us that the distance from an optimal point and the value of the cost function are not strongly correlated. The latter may substantially increase SA run-times.

6.7 Conclusion

In this chapter, we have derived a sufficient (albeit not necessary) condition to test schedulability of recurring real-time tasks under static priority scheduling. It was shown that this condition can be tested in pseudo-polynomial time, provided that task execution requirements and inter-triggering separations have integral values. Furthermore, these results were not too pessimistic and had also practical value. The latter was demonstrated in terms of experiments performed with different task systems, where in each case, an optimal solution for a given problem specification could be reported within reasonable time.

As already mentioned at the beginning of this chapter, we still need to incorporate these results into Sesame by equipping it with a real-time global scheduler. This will eventually allow Sesame to extend its application domain to include real-time multimedia applications. It will then be possible to estimate the real-time performance of those applications, such as video conferencing and HDTV, within the Sesame framework.

7

Conclusion

System-level modeling and early design space exploration plays an increasingly important role in embedded systems design. In Chapter 2 of this thesis, we presented the Sesame software framework [23], [78] for the efficient system-level performance evaluation and architecture exploration of heterogeneous embedded systems targeting the multimedia application domain. We discussed that Sesame provides the designer with an environment which makes it possible to construct architecture (performance) models at the system-level, map applications onto architecture models using analytical modeling and multiobjective optimization methods, perform architectural design space exploration through high-level system simulations, and gradually lower the abstraction level in the high-level architecture models by incorporating more implementation models into them to attain higher accuracy in performance evaluations. In order to realize all these, Sesame closely followed the Y-chart design methodology [4], [56] which separates behavior from implementation by recognizing a distinct model for each within a system specification. The discussion on Sesame contained its three-layer structure, the trace-driven co-simulation technique employed, the application and architecture simulators, and the mapping decision support provided to the designer.

We focused on the problem of *design space pruning and exploration* in Chapter 3. We employed analytical modeling and multiobjective search techniques to prune the prominently large design space during the mapping stage in Sesame. This procedure identified a number of Pareto-optimal solutions which were subsequently simulated by Sesame's software framework for system-level performance evaluation. Combining analytical methods with simulation allowed us to perform fast and accurate design space exploration. We concluded the chapter with experiments, where we pruned and explored the design space of two multimedia applications.

Gradual model refinement was realized within the Sesame framework in Chapter 4. For this purpose, we defined traces and trace transformations which formed the formal underpinnings of the model refinement. Then, we proposed a new mapping strategy which utilized dataflow actors and networks at the intermediate mapping layer in order to implement the aforementioned refinement defined by the trace transformations. The chapter was concluded with an illustrative case study.

In Chapter 5, performing two case studies on a multimedia application which combined methods and tools from Chapters 2, 3, and 4, we first pruned and explored the design space of an M-JPEG encoder application which was mapped onto a platform SoC architecture. We then further refined one of the processing cores of the SoC architecture, using the dataflow-based architecture model refinement technique from Chapter 3. In the second case study, we showed how *model calibration and validation* could be performed using Sesame in combination with other tool-sets from the Artemis project. For this purpose, the M-JPEG encoder was mapped onto the Molen calibration platform [100], a processor–co-processor architecture realized in the Xilinx Vertex II Pro platform, using the Compaan [57] and Laura [106] tool-sets, successively. Using Sesame, we modeled the real Molen platform at the system-level and calibrated these high-level models with low level information. The validation experiments which compared Sesame's system-level models against the real Molen implementation revealed that the Sesame's high-level performance estimations were highly accurate.

Finally, we focused on *real-time issues* in Chapter 6. More specifically, we summarized the recurring real-time task model and derived a scheduling test condition for static priority schedulers to schedule these tasks on a uniprocessor. After summarizing the state-of-the-art for dynamic schedulers, we concluded the chapter with experiments, where a number of task systems were shown to be schedulable under a certain static priority assignment. The latter was located by a simulated annealing search framework.

Future work. The work in this thesis has described research that is still in progress. There exist many opportunities for further research, especially in terms of extensions to the Sesame framework. For example, at the application model layer, in addition to (Kahn) process networks, applications specified in other models of computations can be supported. The architecture model library can be extended to include additional processor, memory, and interconnect models at multiple levels of abstraction. Furthermore, the application events driving the architectural simulation can also be associated with deadlines besides their execution requirements. This would allow architecture models to record any deadline misses, which would help the designer to some extent examine the real-time behavior.

A

Performance metrics

Table A.1 presents the mean values and the standard deviations for the three metrics obtained in the M-JPEG encoder and JPEG decoder case studies in Chapter 3. Best values are shown in bold.

Table A.1: Performance comparison of the MOEAs for the M-JPEG encoder and JPEG decoder applications. Best values are in bold.

		M-JPEG encoder						JPEG decoder					
MOEA	T	D-metric		Δ-metric		∇-metric		D-metric		Δ-metric		∇-metric	
		avg.	std. dev.	avg.	std. dev.	avg.	std. dev.	avg.	std. dev.	avg.	std. dev.	avg.	std. dev.
SPEA2		9.07e-2	2.77e-2	4.55e-2	1.12e-2	5.22e9	2.58e9	2.86e-1	1.60e-2	4.17e-2	8.19e-3	3.04e10	1.18e10
NSGA-II		9.18e-2	2.25e-2	4.70e-2	1.35e-2	5.47e9	3.01e9	2.85e-1	2.18e-2	4.03e-2	7.60e-3	3.29e10	9.54e9
SPEA2r	50	**9.94e-3**	8.93e-3	5.95e-2	1.15e-2	**4.15e10**	8.65e9	**1.36e-1**	2.54e-2	5.30e-2	8.10e-3	**2.03e11**	3.75e10
NSGA-IIr		1.30e-2	1.28e-2	5.97e-2	1.05e-2	3.82e10	9.55e9	1.40e-1	1.62e-2	5.24e-2	5.58e-3	1.93e11	2.33e10
SPEA2R		1.93e-2	2.27e-2	**3.68e-2**	7.27e-3	4.84e9	2.37e9	1.71e-1	1.74e-2	**3.98e-2**	5.12e-3	5.39e10	1.41e10
NSGA-IIR		2.00e-2	2.26e-2	3.79e-2	6.27e-3	5.17e9	1.63e9	1.74e-1	1.57e-2	4.24e-2	5.51e-3	5.75e10	2.02e10
SPEA2		8.74e-2	2.54e-2	4.52e-2	1.23e-2	6.84e9	4.15e9	2.78e-1	1.80e-2	**3.97e-2**	7.47e-3	3.55e10	1.02e10
NSGA-II		8.10e-2	1.81e-2	4.88e-2	9.81e-3	6.17e9	2.17e9	2.82e-1	1.87e-2	**3.97e-2**	7.83e-3	3.48e10	1.16e10
SPEA2r	100	6.50e-3	1.01e-2	6.06e-2	1.19e-2	**4.33e10**	9.71e9	1.34e-1	2.47e-2	5.26e-2	6.95e-3	**2.11e11**	4.00e10
NSGA-IIr		**5.41e-3**	8.41e-3	5.94e-2	8.44e-3	3.97e10	8.59e9	1.39e-1	1.94e-2	5.33e-2	5.51e-3	2.08e11	3.64e10
SPEA2R		5.90e-3	1.15e-2	**4.17e-2**	6.30e-3	4.95e9	1.78e9	1.25e-1	2.02e-2	4.36e-2	4.53e-3	7.72e10	2.09e10
NSGA-IIR		7.32e-3	1.64e-2	4.22e-2	5.26e-3	5.40e9	1.56e9	**1.12e-1**	2.20e-2	4.60e-2	4.68e-3	1.06e11	3.25e10
SPEA2		8.65e-2	2.12e-2	4.82e-2	1.05e-2	6.18e9	1.86e9	2.73e-1	2.27e-2	3.90e-2	8.15e-3	3.78e10	1.44e10
NSGA-II		8.01e-2	1.68e-2	4.61e-2	1.16e-2	6.40e9	1.65e9	2.74e-1	2.18e-3	**3.52e-2**	6.18e-3	3.11e10	9.54e9
SPEA2r	200	5.55e-3	1.06e-2	6.06e-2	1.16e-2	**4.45e10**	9.57e9	1.21e-1	2.30e-2	5.27e-2	7.18e-3	**2.29e11**	4.38e10
NSGA-IIr		4.01e-3	8.00e-3	5.87e-2	8.68e-3	3.97e10	9.61e9	1.32e-1	2.31e-2	5.40e-2	5.92e-3	2.14e11	4.02e10
SPEA2R		9.85e-4	2.29e-3	**4.46e-2**	3.45e-3	5.48e9	1.49e9	**6.25e-2**	1.79e-2	4.75e-2	5.23e-3	1.11e11	2.91e10
NSGA-IIR		**5.50e-4**	2.08e-3	4.51e-2	3.30e-3	5.94e9	8.62e8	6.28e-2	1.71e-2	4.71e-2	4.03e-3	1.41e11	3.57e10

Table A.1: Performance comparison of the MOEAs for the M-JPEG encoder and JPEG decoder applications. Best values are in bold. (*continued*)

		M-JPEG encoder						JPEG decoder					
		D-metric		Δ-metric		∇-metric		D-metric		Δ-metric		∇-metric	
MOEA	T	avg.	std. dev.	avg.	std. dev.	avg.	std. dev.	avg.	std. dev.	avg.	std. dev.	avg.	std. dev.
SPEA2	300	8.26e-2	1.98e-2	5.03e-2	1.30e-2	6.77e9	2.05e9	2.76e-1	2.21e-2	3.68e-2	8.56e-3	3.27e10	1.15e10
NSGA-II	300	8.64e-2	2.15e-2	5.02e-2	1.41e-2	6.69e9	1.70e9	2.87e-1	1.96e-2	**3.55e-2**	5.66e-3	3.19e10	8.27e9
SPEA2r	300	4.20e-3	8.58e-3	5.94e-2	1.02e-2	**4.45e10**	9.91e9	1.08e-1	3.19e-2	5.42e-2	7.35e-3	**2.48e11**	4.82e10
NSGA-IIr	300	3.67e-3	8.34e-3	5.71e-2	8.77e-3	3.93e10	9.73e9	1.29e-1	2.71e-2	5.34e-2	6.68e-3	2.24e11	5.16e10
SPEA2R	300	3.49e-5	1.91e-4	**4.60e-2**	1.16e-3	5.78e9	9.80e8	**3.82e-2**	1.61e-2	4.99e-2	4.72e-3	1.27e11	2.38e10
NSGA-IIR	300	**1.37e-5**	7.52e-5	**4.60e-2**	1.17e-3	5.99e9	5.92e8	4.42e-2	2.02e-2	4.34e-2	5.66e-3	1.47e11	2.65e10
SPEA2	500	8.63e-2	2.31e-2	5.07e-2	1.46e-2	7.25e9	3.16e9	2.81e-1	2.22e-2	3.35e-2	7.34e-3	3.05e10	8.73e9
NSGA-II	500	8.58e-2	1.81e-2	4.81e-2	1.31e-2	7.23e9	1.47e9	2.91e-1	2.01e-2	**3.25e-2**	6.79e-3	2.59e10	1.04e10
SPEA2r	500	2.55e-3	7.19e-3	5.99e-2	1.02e-2	**4.50e10**	1.15e10	9.18e-2	3.32e-2	5.58e-2	8.17e-3	**2.65e11**	4.30e10
NSGA-IIr	500	2.52e-3	4.81e-3	5.85e-2	7.79e-3	3.90e10	9.53e9	1.16e-1	3.30e-2	5.28e-2	8.29e-3	2.58e11	7.30e10
SPEA2R	500	3.49e-5	1.91e-4	4.60e-2	1.12e-3	5.99e9	5.79e8	**2.04e-2**	1.36e-2	5.15e-2	4.75e-3	1.34e11	1.97e10
NSGA-IIR	500	**0.00e0**	0.00e0	**4.59e-2**	1.20e-3	6.09e9	4.27e7	2.25e-2	1.67e-2	4.37e-2	5.01e-3	1.56e11	2.61e10
SPEA2	1000	9.10e-2	1.82e-2	4.98e-2	1.22e-2	7.26e9	4.43e9	2.86e-1	2.00e-2	3.34e-2	6.50e-3	2.50e10	8.76e9
NSGA-II	1000	7.74e-2	1.44e-2	4.77e-2	9.89e-3	7.59e9	4.44e9	2.94e-1	2.04e-2	**3.05e-2**	6.86e-3	2.51e10	9.26e9
SPEA2r	1000	2.02e-4	6.77e-4	5.96e-2	1.04e-2	**4.37e10**	1.17e10	5.18e-2	3.08e-2	5.76e-2	7.44e-3	3.12e11	6.76e10
NSGA-IIr	1000	2.09e-3	4.90e-3	6.05e-2	9.55e-3	3.92e10	9.68e9	6.70e-2	4.04e-2	5.56e-2	1.25e-2	**3.17e11**	8.82e10
SPEA2R	1000	3.38e-5	1.85e-4	4.59e-2	1.13e-3	6.09e9	3.55e7	**9.43e-3**	3.83e-3	5.17e-2	4.63e-3	1.55e11	1.97e10
NSGA-IIR	1000	**0.00e0**	0.00e0	**4.58e-2**	9.56e-4	6.09e9	3.55e7	1.27e-2	9.33e-3	4.34e-2	5.07e-3	1.69e11	1.84e10

B

Task systems

Original task graphs for tasks used in the experiments in Chapter 6 are given in Figure B.1. In all task graphs, a vertex with no incoming edge is a source vertex, and similarly a vertex with no outgoing edge is a sink vertex. In the recurring real-time task model, tasks have single source and sink vertices in their task graphs and transforming such a task graph was already shown in Figure 2. However as seen in Figure B.1, a number of tasks taken from the literature were defined in earlier task models and they have multiple source and/or sink vertices. In Figure B.2, we show how these task graphs are transformed so that the transformed task graphs have single source and sink vertices. There exist three different cases: (1) tasks with multiple sink vertices, (2) tasks with multiple source vertices, and (3) tasks with multiple source *and* sink vertices. In Figures B.2(a), B.2(b) and B.2(c), one example of a transformed task graph is given for each case.

Alternative to the examples in Figure B.2, we could also add dummy vertices to original task graphs and subsequently use the standard procedure (explained in Section 6.2.2) to transform them. However, this would unnecessarily increase the number of dummy vertices in the transformed task graphs, which in turn would increase run-times for $T.rbf(t)$ calculations.

Although not explicitly mentioned previously, it should be clear from its input that Algorithm 2 actually operates on the original task graphs. Hence, the schedulability condition is tested only once for all vertices (i.e. subtasks) on each iteration of the algorithm.

Finally, in Table B.1 we provide values used in the experiments for each task system that we have synthesized using tasks in Figure B.1. The values are given

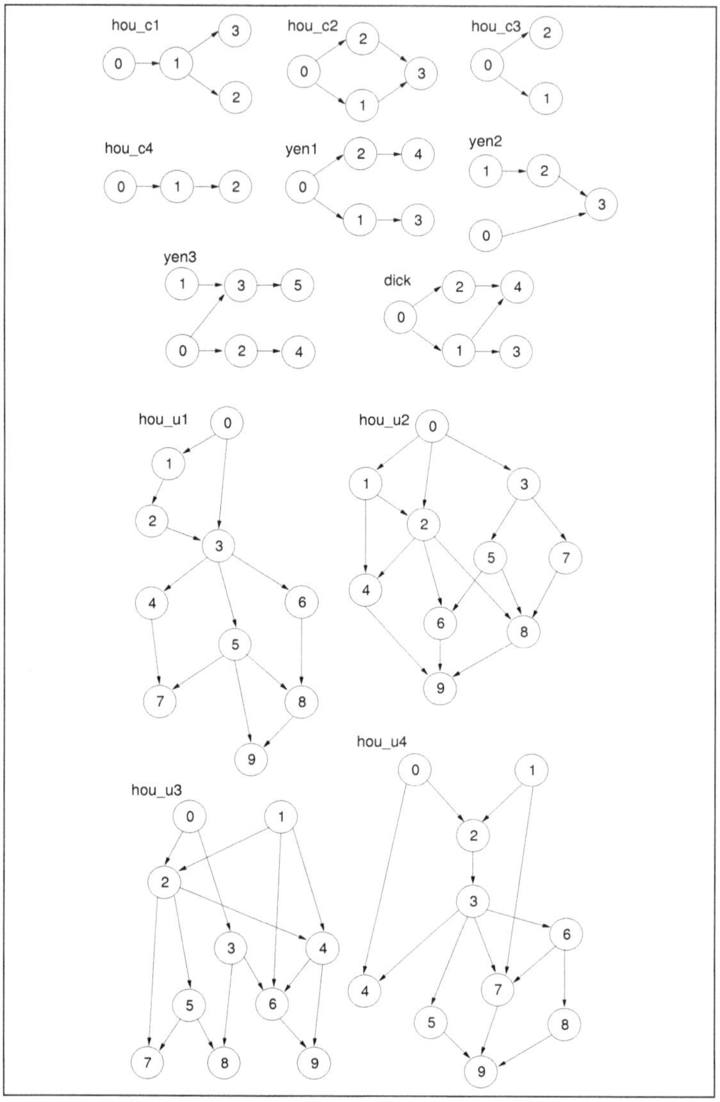

Figure B.1: Original task graphs taken from the literature. Some of the task graphs have multiple source and/or sink vertices.

with respect to original task graphs rather than transformed task graphs. In addition, we should also note that during all experiments, inter-triggering separations were set equal to deadlines, i.e. $p(u, v) = d(u)$ for all $u, v \in T$ in all task systems.

Table B.1: Experimental Data

T	v	$e(v)$							
		TS1	TS2	TS3	TS4	TS5	TS6	TS7	$d(v)$
hou_c1	0	7	3	6	5	5	5	5	71
	1	9	5	6	5	5	4	5	56
	2	10	6	6	5	5	4	5	63
	3	4	1	1	1	3	1	3	50
hou_c2	0	5	4	2	2	3	4	3	80
	1	8	7	6	5	5	4	5	99
	2	10	9	6	5	4	6	5	99
	3	10	9	5	4	3	2	2	46
hou_c3	0	6	5	8	5	4	5	4	64
	1	8	6	5	4	6	2	3	93
	2	10	9	8	5	4	4	4	53
hou_c4	0	4	4	5	4	5	6	4	78
	1	8	8	5	4	5	4	4	74
	2	8	7	5	3	4	3	4	57
yen1	0	1	6	6	5	5	5	4	73
	1	1	1	1	1	3	1	3	72
	2	6	4	6	5	5	5	4	82
	3	8	6	6	5	4	4	4	82
	4	8	6	6	5	4	5	4	77
yen2	0	9	7	6	6	5	4	2	80
	1	9	7	6	6	4	3	3	57
	2	8	6	5	5	4	4	3	66
	3	8	6	6	6	4	3	3	61
yen3	0	-	4	4	4	4	2	4	53
	1	-	5	5	5	4	4	4	61
	2	-	2	2	2	3	1	5	89
	3	-	6	6	5	5	4	5	82
	4	-	1	1	1	2	1	5	97
	5	-	4	4	4	3	2	3	32
dick	0	-	-	4	4	4	2	3	96
	1	-	-	5	5	2	3	3	48
	2	-	-	7	6	3	4	4	59
	3	-	-	7	6	3	4	4	85
	4	-	-	3	3	1	1	1	36
hou_u1	0	-	-	-	4	4	4	3	58
	1	-	-	-	6	5	4	4	98
	2	-	-	-	2	2	2	3	52
	3	-	-	-	1	3	1	3	59
	4	-	-	-	1	3	1	1	64
	5	-	-	-	1	1	1	1	62
	6	-	-	-	4	5	4	4	88
	7	-	-	-	4	4	4	2	63
	8	-	-	-	4	4	4	3	68
	9	-	-	-	5	5	4	3	54

Table B.1: Experimental Data *(continued)*

		$e(v)$							
T	v	TS1	TS2	TS3	TS4	TS5	TS6	TS7	$d(v)$
hou_u2	0	-	-	-	-	4	4	4	85
	1	-	-	-	-	3	1	1	89
	2	-	-	-	-	3	3	2	66
	3	-	-	-	-	4	4	4	78
	4	-	-	-	-	4	4	3	97
	5	-	-	-	-	3	1	1	80
	6	-	-	-	-	3	3	2	74
	7	-	-	-	-	4	4	4	82
	8	-	-	-	-	4	4	4	56
	9	-	-	-	-	6	4	4	95
hou_u3	0	-	-	-	-	-	4	4	72
	1	-	-	-	-	-	1	1	62
	2	-	-	-	-	-	4	4	92
	3	-	-	-	-	-	2	1	88
	4	-	-	-	-	-	4	4	81
	5	-	-	-	-	-	4	3	85
	6	-	-	-	-	-	4	4	86
	7	-	-	-	-	-	2	1	95
	8	-	-	-	-	-	3	2	70
	9	-	-	-	-	-	4	4	77
hou_u4	0	-	-	-	-	-	-	1	71
	1	-	-	-	-	-	-	4	80
	2	-	-	-	-	-	-	4	96
	3	-	-	-	-	-	-	4	72
	4	-	-	-	-	-	-	2	78
	5	-	-	-	-	-	-	1	96
	6	-	-	-	-	-	-	4	82
	7	-	-	-	-	-	-	3	68
	8	-	-	-	-	-	-	4	97
	9	-	-	-	-	-	-	3	91

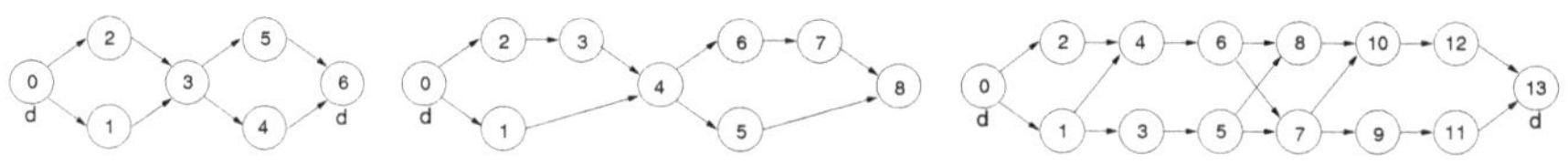

(a) Case 1: Task with multiple sink vertices.

(b) Case 2: Task with multiple source vertices.

(c) Case 3: Task with multiple source *and* sink vertices.

Figure B.2: Three example transformed task graphs for tasks with multiple source and/or sink vertices. In all transformed task graphs, dummy vertices added are labeled with "d". (a) Transformed task graph for hou_c3 which has multiple sink vertices. (b) Transformed task graph for yen2 which has multiple source vertices. (c) Transformed task graph for yen3 which has multiple source and sink vertices.

References

[1] G. Alpaydin, S. Balkir, and G. Dundar. An evolutionary approach to automatic synthesis of high-performance analog integrated circuits. *IEEE Transactions on Evolutionary Computation*, 7(3):240–252, 2003.

[2] G. Ascia, V. Catania, and M. Palesi. A GA-based design space exploration framework for parameterized system-on-a-chip platforms. *IEEE Transactions on Evolutionary Computation*, 8(4):329–346, 2004.

[3] T. Austin, E. Larson, and D. Ernst. SimpleScalar: An infrastructure for computer system modeling. *IEEE Computer*, 35(2):59–67, Feb. 2002.

[4] F. Balarin, E. Sentovich, M. Chiodo, P. Giusto, H. Hsieh, B. Tabbara, A. Jurecska, L. Lavagno, C. Passerone, K. Suzuki, and A. Sangiovanni-Vincentelli. *Hardware-Software Co-design of Embedded Systems – The POLIS approach.* Kluwer Academic Publishers, 1997.

[5] F. Balarin, Y. Watanabe, H. Hsieh, L. Lavagno, C. Passerone, and A. Sangiovanni-Vincentelli. Metropolis: An integrated electronic system design environment. *Computer*, 36(4):45–52, 2003.

[6] S. K. Baruah. Feasibility analysis of recurring branching tasks. In *Proc. of the Euromicro Workshop on Real-Time Systems*, pages 138–145, June 1998.

[7] S. K. Baruah. A general model for recurring real-time tasks. In *Proc. of the Real Time Systems Symposium*, pages 114–122, Dec. 1998.

[8] S. K. Baruah. Dynamic- and static-priority scheduling of recurring real-time tasks. *Real-Time Systems*, 24(1):93–128, 2003.

[9] S. K. Baruah, D. Chen, S. Gorinsky, and A. K. Mok. Generalized multiframe tasks. *Real-Time Systems*, 17(1):5–22, 1999.

[10] M. Bauer and W. Ecker. Hardware/software co-simulation in a VHDL-based test bench approach. In *Proc. of the Design Automation Conference*, pages 774–779, 1997.

[11] D. Beasley, D. Bull, and R. Martin. An overview of genetic algorithms: Part 1, fundamentals. *University Computing*, 15(2):58–69, 1993.

[12] S. Bleuler, M. Laumanns, L. Thiele, and E. Zitzler. PISA – a platform and programming language independent interface for search algorithms. In C. M. Fonseca, P. J. Fleming, E. Zitzler, K. Deb, and L. Thiele, editors, *Evolutionary Multi-Criterion Optimization (EMO 2003)*, volume 2632 of *LNCS*, pages 494–508. Springer-Verlag, 2003.

[13] T. Blickle, J. Teich, and L. Thiele. System-level synthesis using evolutionary algorithms. *Design Automation for Embedded Systems*, 3(1):23–58, 1998.

[14] M. S. Bright and T. Arslan. Synthesis of low-power DSP systems using a genetic algorithm. *IEEE Transactions on Evolutionary Computation*, 5(1):27–40, 2001.

[15] J. T. Buck. *Scheduling Dynamic Dataflow Graphs with Bounded Memory using the Token Flow Model.* PhD thesis, Dept. of Electrical Engineering and Computer Sciences, University of California, Berkeley, 1993.

[16] J. T. Buck. Static scheduling and code generation from dynamic dataflow graphs with integer valued control streams. In *Proc. of the 28th Asilomar conference on Signals, Systems, and Computers*, pages 508–513, Oct. 1994.

[17] L. Cai and D. Gajski. Transaction level modeling: An overview. In *Proc. of the Int. Conference on Hardware/Software Codesign and System Synthesis*, pages 19–24, Oct. 2003.

[18] S. Chakraborty, T. Erlebach, S. Künzli, and L. Thiele. Approximate schedulability analysis. In *Proc. of IEEE Real-Time Systems Symposium*, pages 159–168, Dec. 2002.

[19] S. Chakraborty, T. Erlebach, S. Künzli, and L. Thiele. Schedulability of event-driven code blocks in real-time embedded systems. In *Proc. of the Design Automation Conference*, pages 616–621, June 2002.

[20] S. Chakraborty, T. Erlebach, and L. Thiele. On the complexity of scheduling conditional real-time code. In *Proc. of the 7th Int. Workshop on Algorithms and Data Structures*, volume 2125 of *LNCS*, pages 38–49. Springer-Verlag, 2001.

[21] C. A. Coello Coello. Guest editorial: Special issue on evolutionary multiobjective optimization. *IEEE Transactions on Evolutionary Computation*, 7(2):97–99, 2003.

[22] C. A. Coello Coello, D. A. Van Veldhuizen, and G. B. Lamont. *Evolutionary Algorithms for Solving Multi-Objective Problems*. Kluwer Academic Publishers, 2002.

[23] J. E. Coffland and A. D. Pimentel. A software framework for efficient system-level performance evaluation of embedded systems. In *Proc. of the ACM Symposium on Applied Computing*, pages 666–671, Mar. 2003. `http://sesamesim.sourceforge.net/`.

[24] S. M. Coumeri and D. E. Thomas. A simulation environment for hardware-software codesign. In *Proc. of the Int. Conference on Computer Design*, pages 58–63, 1995.

[25] ILOG CPLEX, `http://www.ilog.com/products/cplex`.

[26] E. A. de Kock. Multiprocessor mapping of process networks: A JPEG decoding case study. In *Proc. of Int. Symposium on System Synthesis*, pages 68–73, Oct. 2002.

[27] E. A. de Kock, G. Essink, W. Smits, P. van der Wolf, J. Brunel, W. Kruijtzer, P. Lieverse, and K. Vissers. YAPI: Application modeling for signal processing systems. In *Proc. of the Design Automation Conference*, pages 402–405, June 2000.

[28] K. Deb. *Multi-Objective Optimization Using Evolutionary Algorithms*. John Wiley & Sons, 2001.

[29] K. Deb, S. Agrawal, A. Pratap, and T. Meyarivan. A fast elitist non-dominated sorting genetic algorithm for multi-objective optimization: NSGA-II. In M. Schoenauer, K. Deb, G. Rudolph, X. Yao, E. Lutton, J. Merelo, and H. Schwefel, editors, *Parallel Problem Solving from Nature – PPSN VI*, pages 849–858. Springer, 2000.

[30] R. P. Dick and N. K. Jha. MOGAC: A multiobjective genetic algorithm for hardware-software co-synthesis of distributed embedded systems. *IEEE Transactions on Computer-Aided Design of Integrated Circuits and Systems*, 17(10):920–935, Oct. 1998.

[31] R. P. Dick and N. K. Jha. MOCSYN: Multiobjective core-based single-chip system synthesis. In *Proc. of the Design, Automation and Test in Europe*, pages 263–270, Mar. 1999.

[32] M. Ehrgott. *Multicriteria Optimization*. Lecture Notes in Economics and Mathematical Systems. Springer-Verlag, 2000.

[33] J. Eker, J. Janneck, E. A. Lee, J. Liu, X. Liu, J. Ludvig, S. Neuendorffer, S. Sachs, and Y. Xiong. Taming heterogeneity – the Ptolemy approach. *Proceedings of the IEEE*, 91(1):127–144, Jan. 2003.

[34] C. Erbas, S. Cerav-Erbas, and A. D. Pimentel. Static priority scheduling of event-triggered real-time embedded systems. *Formal Methods in System Design*. Special issue on best papers of MEMOCODE'04. (In press).

[35] C. Erbas, S. Cerav-Erbas, and A. D. Pimentel. A multiobjective optimization model for exploring multiprocessor mappings of process networks. In *Proc. of the Int. Conference on Hardware/Software Codesign and System Synthesis*, pages 182–187, Oct. 2003.

[36] C. Erbas, S. Cerav-Erbas, and A. D. Pimentel. Static priority scheduling of event-triggered real-time embedded systems. In *Proc. of the Int. Conference on Formal Methods and Models for Codesign*, pages 109–118, June 2004.

[37] C. Erbas, S. Cerav-Erbas, and A. D. Pimentel. Multiobjective optimization and evolutionary algorithms for the application mapping problem in multiprocessor system-on-chip design. *IEEE Transactions on Evolutionary Computation*, 10(3):358–374, June 2006.

[38] C. Erbas and A. D. Pimentel. Utilizing synthesis methods in accurate system-level exploration of heterogeneous embedded systems. In *Proc. of the IEEE Workshop on Signal Processing Systems*, pages 310–315, Aug. 2003.

[39] C. Erbas, A. D. Pimentel, M. Thompson, and S. Polstra. A framework for system-level modeling and simulation of embedded systems architectures. Submitted for publication.

[40] C. Erbas, S. Polstra, and A. D. Pimentel. IDF models for trace transformations: A case study in computational refinement. In A. Pimentel and S. Vassiliadis, editors, *Computer Systems: Architectures, Modeling, and Simulation*, volume 3133 of *LNCS*, pages 178–187. Springer-Verlag, 2003.

[41] C. M. Fonseca and P. J. Flemming. Genetic algorithms for multiobjective optimization: Formulation, discussion and generalization. In *Proc. of the Int. Conference on Genetic Algorithms*, pages 416–423, 1993.

[42] J. C. Gallagher, S. Vigraham, and G. Kramer. A family of compact genetic algorithms for intrinsic evolvable hardware. *IEEE Transactions on Evolutionary Computation*, 8(2):111–126, 2004.

[43] M. Geilen and T. Basten. Requirements on the execution of Kahn process networks. In *Proc. of the 12th European Symposium on Programming*, volume 2618 of *LNCS*, pages 319–334. Springer, 2003.

[44] T. Givargis and F. Vahid. Platune: A tuning framework for system-on-a-chip platforms. *IEEE Transactions on Computer-Aided Design of Integrated Circuits and Systems*, 21(11):1317–1327, 2002.

[45] T. Givargis, F. Vahid, and J. Henkel. System-level exploration for pareto-optimal configurations in parameterized system-on-a-chip. *IEEE Transactions on Very Large Scale Integration (VLSI) Systems*, 10(4):416–422, 2002.

[46] D. E. Goldberg. *Genetic Algorithms in Search, Optimization, and Machine Learning*. Addison-Wesley, 1989.

[47] M. Gries and K. Keutzer. *Building ASIPs: The Mescal Methodology*. Springer, 2005.

[48] A. Hamann, M. Jersak, K. Richter, and R. Ernst. A framework for modular analysis and exploration of heterogeneous embedded systems. *Real-Time Systems*, 35(1–3):101–137, July 2006.

[49] K. Hines and G. Borriello. Dynamic communication models in embedded system co-simulation. In *Proc. of the Design Automation Conference*, pages 395–400, 1997.

[50] J. Hou and W. Wolf. Process partitioning for distributed embedded systems. In *Proc. of Int. Workshop on Hardware/Software Codesign*, pages 70–76, Mar. 1996.

[51] J. Hromkovic. *Algorithmics for Hard Problems (Introduction to Combinatorial Optimization, Randomization, Approximation, and Heuristics)*. Springer-Verlag, 2002.

[52] A. J. Gadient J. A. Debardelaben, V. K. Madisetti. Incorporating cost modeling in embedded-system design. *IEEE Design and Test of Computers*, 14(3):24–35, 1997.

[53] M. T. Jensen. Reducing the run-time complexity of multi-objective eas: The nsga-ii and other algorithms. *IEEE Transactions on Evolutionary Computation*, 7(5):503–515, 2003.

[54] G. Kahn. The semantics of a simple language for parallel programming. In *Proc. of the IFIP Congress*, pages 471–475, 1974.

[55] K. Keutzer, S. Malik, R. Newton, J. Rabaey, and A. Sangiovanni-Vincentelli. System level design: Orthogonalization of concerns and platform-based design. *IEEE Transactions on Computer-Aided Design of Circuits and Systems*, 19(12):1523–1543, 2000.

[56] B. Kienhuis, E. Deprettere, K. Vissers, and P. van der Wolf. An approach for quantitative analysis of application-specific dataflow architectures. In *Proc. of the Int. Conf. Application-specific Systems, Architectures and Processors*, pages 338–349, 1997.

[57] B. Kienhuis, E. Rijpkema, and E. Deprettere. Compaan: Deriving process networks from matlab for embedded signal processing architectures. In *Proc. of the Int. Workshop on Hardware/Software Codesign*, pages 13–17, 2000.

[58] Y. Kim, K. Kim, Y. Shin, T. Ahn, W. Sung, K. Choi, and S. Ha. An integrated hardware-software cosimulation environment for heterogeneous systems prototyping. In *Proc. of the Conference Asia South Pacific Design Automation*, pages 101–106, 1995.

[59] J. Knowles and D. Corne. On metrics for comparing non-dominated sets. In *Proc. of the Congress on Evolutionary Computation*, pages 711–716, May 2002.

[60] T. Kogel, M. Doerper, A. Wieferink, S. Goossens, R. Leupers, G. Ascheid, and H. Meyr. A modular simulation framework for architectural exploration of on-chip interconnection networks. In *Proc. of the Int. Conference on Hardware/Software Codesign and System Synthesis*, pages 7–12, Oct. 2003.

[61] M. Laumanns, E. Zitzler, and L. Thiele. A unified model for multi-objective evolutionary algorithms with elitism. In *Proc. of the Congress on Evolutionary Computation*, pages 46–53, 2000.

[62] E. A. Lee and D. G. Messerschmitt. Synchronous Data Flow. *Proc. of the IEEE*, 75(9):1235–1245, 1987.

[63] E. A. Lee and T. M. Parks. Dataflow process networks. *Proc. of the IEEE*, 83(5):773–799, 1995.

[64] E. A. Lee and A. Sangiovanni-Vincentelli. A framework for comparing models of computation. *IEEE Trans. Computer-Aided Design of Integrated Circuits and Systems*, 17(12):1217–1229, Dec. 1998.

[65] P. Lieverse, T. Stefanov, P. van der Wolf, and E. Deprettere. System level design with Spade: an M-JPEG case study. In *Proc. of the Int. Conference on Computer Aided Design*, pages 31–38, Nov. 2001.

[66] P. Lieverse, P. van der Wolf, and E. Deprettere. A trace transformation technique for communication refinement. In *Proc. of the 9th Int. Symposium on Hardware/Software Codesign*, pages 134–139, Apr. 2001.

[67] P. Lieverse, P. van der Wolf, E. Deprettere, and K. Vissers. A methodology for architecture exploration of heterogeneous signal processing systems. *Journal of VLSI Signal Processing for Signal, Image and Video Technology*, 29(3):197–207, 2001.

[68] C. Liu and J. Layland. Scheduling algorithms for multiprogramming in a hard-real-time environment. *Journal of the ACM*, 20(1):46–61, 1973.

[69] H. Lu and G. G. Yen. Rank-density-based multiobjective genetic algorithm and benchmark test function study. *IEEE Transactions on Evolutionary Computation*, 7(4):325–343, 2003.

[70] S. Mohanty and V. Prasanna. Rapid system-level performance evaluation and optimization for application mapping onto SoC architectures. In *Proc. of the IEEE ASIC/SOC Conference*, pages 160–167, 2002.

[71] A. K. Mok. *Fundamental Design Problems of Distributed Systems for the Hard-Real-Time Environment.* PhD thesis, Department of Electrical Engineering and Computer Science, Massachusetts Institute of Technology, 1983.

[72] A. K. Mok and D. Chen. A multiframe model for real-time tasks. *IEEE Trans. on Software Engineering*, 23(10):635–645, 1997.

[73] H. Muller. *Simulating Computer Architectures.* PhD thesis, Department of Computer Science, University of Amsterdam, 1993.

[74] T. M. Parks. *Bounded Scheduling of Process Networks.* PhD thesis, Department of Electrical Engineering and Computer Sciences, University of California, Berkeley, 1995.

[75] J. M. Paul, D. E. Thomas, and A. S. Cassidy. High-level modeling and simulation of single-chip programmable heterogeneous multiprocessors. *ACM Transactions on Design Automation of Embedded Systems*, 10(3):431–461, July 2005.

[76] A. D. Pimentel. The Artemis workbench for system-level performance evaluation of embedded systems. *Int. Journal of Embedded Systems.* To be published.

[77] A. D. Pimentel and C. Erbas. An IDF-based trace transformation method for communication refinement. In *Proc. of the Design Automation Conference*, pages 402–407, June 2003.

[78] A. D. Pimentel, C. Erbas, and S. Polstra. A systematic approach to exploring embedded system architectures at multiple abstraction levels. *IEEE Transactions on Computers*, 55(2):99–112, 2006.

[79] A. D. Pimentel, P. Lieverse, P. van der Wolf, L. O. Hertzberger, and E. Deprettere. Exploring embedded-systems architectures with Artemis. *Computer*, 34(11):57–63, Nov. 2001.

[80] A. D. Pimentel, S. Polstra, F. Terpstra, A. W. van Halderen, J. E. Coffland, and L. O. Hertzberger. Towards efficient design space exploration of heterogeneous embedded media systems. In E. Deprettere, J. Teich, and S. Vassiliadis, editors, *Embedded Processor Design Challenges: Systems, Architectures, Modeling, and Simulation*, volume 2268 of *LNCS*, pages 57–73. Springer-Verlag, 2002.

[81] A. D. Pimentel, F. Terpstra, S. Polstra, and J. E. Coffland. On the modeling of intra-task parallelism in task-level parallel embedded systems. In S. Bhattacharyya, E. Deprettere, and J. Teich, editors, *Domain-Specific Processors: Systems, Architectures, Modeling, and Simulation*, pages 85–105. Marcel Dekker Inc., 2003.

[82] P. Pop, P. Eles, and Z. Peng. Schedulability analysis for systems with data and control dependencies. In *Proc. of Euromicro Conference on Real-Time Systems*, pages 201–208, June 2000.

[83] T. Pop, P. Eles, and Z. Peng. Schedulability analysis for distributed heterogeneous time/event-triggered real-time systems. In *Proc. of Euromicro Conference on Real-Time Systems*, pages 257–266, July 2003.

[84] G. Rudolph. Evolutionary search under partially ordered fitness sets. In M. F. Sebaaly, editor, *Proc. of the Int. NAISO Congress on Information Science Innovations*, pages 818–822. ICSC Academic Press, 2001.

[85] J. D. Schaffer. Multiple objective optimization with vector evaluated genetic algorithms. In *Proc. of the Int. Conference on Genetic Algorithms*, pages 93–100, 1985.

[86] J. Soininen, T. Huttunen, K. Tiensyrja, and H. Heusala. Cosimulation of real-time control systems. In *Proc. of European Design Automation Conference*, pages 170–175, 1995.

[87] W. Spears. Crossover or mutation? In *Proc. of the Workshop on Foundations of Genetic Algorithms*, pages 221–237, July 1992.

[88] N. Srinivas and K. Deb. Multiobjective optimization using nondominated sorting in genetic algorithms. *Evolutionary Computation*, 2(3):221–248, 1994.

[89] A. Stammermann, L. Kruse, W. Nebel, A. Pratsch, E. Schmidt, M. Schulte, and A. Schulz. System level optimization and design space exploration for low power. In *Proc. of the Int. Symposium on Systems Synthesis*, pages 142–146, Oct. 2001.

[90] T. Stefanov and E. Deprettere. Deriving process networks from weakly dynamic applications in system-level design. In *Proc. of the Int. Conference on Hardware/Software Codesign and System Synthesis*, pages 90–96, Oct. 2003.

[91] R. E. Steuer. An overview in graphs of multiple objective programming. In E. Zitzler, K. Deb, L. Thiele, C. A. Coello Coello, and D. Corne, editors, *Proc. of the Int. Conference on Evolutionary Multi-Criterion Optimization*, volume 1993 of *LNCS*, pages 41–51. Springer-Verlag, 2001.

[92] R. E. Steuer and E. U. Choo. An interactive weighted Tchebycheff procedure for multiple objective programming. *Mathematical Programming*, 26:326–344, 1983.

[93] SystemC, `http://www.systemc.org/`.

[94] G. Syswerda. Uniform crossover in genetic algorithms. In *Proc. of the Int. Conference on Genetic Algorithms*, pages 2–9, 1989.

[95] R. Szymanek, F. Catthoor, and K. Kuchcinski. Time-energy design space exploration for multi-layer memory architectures. In *Proc. of the Design, Automation and Test in Europe*, pages 10318–10323, Feb. 2004.

[96] L. Thiele, S. Chakraborty, M. Gries, and S. Künzli. A framework for evaluating design tradeoffs in packet processing architectures. In *Proc. of the Design Automation Conference*, pages 880–885, June 2002.

[97] M. Thompson and A. D. Pimentel. A high-level programming paradigm for SystemC. In *Proc. of the Int. Workshop on Systems, Architectures, Modeling, and Simulation*, volume 3133 of *LNCS*, pages 530–539. Springer, 2004.

[98] M. Thompson, A. D. Pimentel, S. Polstra, and C. Erbas. A mixed-level co-simulation method for system-level design space exploration. In *Proc. IEEE Workshop on Embedded Systems for Real-Time Multimedia*, Oct. 2006. To appear.

[99] R. Uhlig and T. Mudge. Trace-driven memory simulation: A survey. *ACM Computing Surveys*, 29(2):128–170, 1997.

[100] S. Vassiliadis, S. Wong, G. N. Gaydadjiev, K. Bertels, G. K. Kuzmanov, and E. Moscu-Panainte. The Molen polymorphic processor. *IEEE Transactions on Computers*, 53(11):1363–1375, 2004.

[101] Cadence Design Systems, Inc., http://www.cadence.com/.

[102] M. Wall. *GAlib: A C++ Library of Genetic Algorithm Components*. Massachusetts Institute of Technology, 1996.

[103] W. Wolf. *Computers as Components - A Quantitative Approach*. Morgan Kaufmann Publishers, 2001.

[104] G. G. Yen and L. Haiming. Dynamic multiobjective evolutionary algorithm: Adaptive cell-based rank and density estimation. *IEEE Transactions on Evolutionary Computation*, 7(3):253–274, 2003.

[105] T. Yen and W. Wolf. *Hardware-Software Co-Synthesis of Distributed Embedded Systems.* Kluwer Academic Publishers, 1996.

[106] C. Zissulescu, T. Stefanov, B. Kienhuis, and E. Deprettere. Laura: Leiden architecture research and exploration tool. In J. de Sousa P. Cheung, G. Constantinides, editor, *Proc. of the Int. Conference on Field Programmable Logic and Application*, volume 2778 of *LNCS*, pages 911–920. Springer-Verlag, 2003.

[107] E. Zitzler. *Evolutionary Algorithms for Multiobjective Optimization: Methods and Applications.* PhD thesis, Computer Engineering and Networks Laboratory, Swiss Federal Institute of Technology Zurich, 1999.

[108] E. Zitzler, K. Deb, and L. Thiele. Comparison of multiobjective evolutionary algorithms: Empirical results. *Evolutionary Computation*, 8(2):173–195, 2000.

[109] E. Zitzler, M. Laumanns, and L. Thiele. SPEA2: Improving the strength pareto evolutionary algorithm for multiobjective optimization. In K. Giannakoglou, D. Tsahalis, J. Periaux, K. Papailiou, and T. Fogarty, editors, *Evolutionary Methods for Design, Optimisation, and Control*, pages 95–100. CIMNE, 2002.

[110] V. Zivkovic, P. van der Wolf, E. Deprettere, and E. A. de Kock. Design space exploration of streaming multiprocessor architectures. In *Proc. of the IEEE Workshop on Signal Processing Systems*, pages 228–234, Oct. 2002.

Nederlandse samenvatting

De systeem-niveau modellering en vroegtijdige ontwerpruimte exploratie spelen een steeds belangrijkere rol bij het ontwerpen van embedded systemen. In hoofdstuk 2 van dit proefschrift beschrijven we de Sesame software omgeving voor de efficiënte systeem-niveau evaluatie en architectuur exploratie van de heterogene embedded systemen voor het multimedia applicatie domein. We laten zien dat de ontwerper met Sesame architectuur (performance) modellen op het systeem-niveau kan maken, applicaties op deze architectuur modellen kan afbeelden met behulp van analytische modellering en multi-objectieve optimalisatie methoden, de ontwerpruimte van de architectuur kan exploreren met gebruik van abstracte systeem simulaties, en geleidelijk het abstractie niveau van de architectuur modellen kan verlagen door het toevoegen van informatie over de implementatie waardoor de nauwkeurigheid wordt verhoogd. Sesame volgt de Y-chart ontwerpmethodologie waarin het gedrag en de implementatie van een systeem apart worden gemodelleerd. We beschrijven de drie-lagen structuur van Sesame, de trace-driven co-simulatie, en de applicatie- en architectuur-simulatoren.

In hoofdstuk 3 kijken we naar de methoden voor het reduceren en exploreren van de ontwerpruimte. Het reduceren van de ontwerpruimte doen we met behulp van analytische modellen en multi-objectieve zoektechnieken. Vervolgens vindt de exploratie plaats door de simulatie van de beste kandidaten uit de gereduceerde ontwerpruimte. De combinatie van de analytische methoden en de systeem-niveau simulatie resulteert in een snelle en nauwkeurige performance evaluatie.

Hoofdstuk 4 behandelt de geleidelijke verfijning van de modellen. Deze verfijning wordt gerealiseerd met traces en trace transformaties. Hiervoor introduceren we ook een nieuwe afbeeldingsstrategie waarin deze transformaties worden uitgevoerd. Het hoofdstuk wordt beëindigd met een illustratieve casestudy.

Hoofdstuk 5 presenteert twee casestudies met de Motion-JPEG encoder applicatie waarin de technieken en ideeën vanuit de eerdere hoofdstukken 2, 3, en 4 zijn toegepast. Met behulp van de andere tool-sets uit het Artemis project hebben we onze systeem-niveau modellen gevalideerd.

Tenslotte behandelt hoofdstuk 6 enkele real-time kwesties. Eerst geven we een samenvatting van de "recurring real-time task model" en vervolgens leiden we een scheduling test conditie af voor de statische prioriteit scheduler die het mogelijk maakt om meerdere taken op een processor te schedulen. De experimenten aan het eind van het hoofdstuk met de enkele taak-systemen tonen aan dat de afgeleide scheduling conditie ook in de praktijk werkt.

Scientific output

Journal publications

- C. Erbas, A. D. Pimentel, M. Thompson, and S. Polstra. A Framework for System-level Modeling and Simulation of Embedded Systems Architectures. Submitted for publication.

- C. Erbas, S. Cerav-Erbas, and A. D. Pimentel. Static Priority Scheduling of Event-Triggered Real-Time Embedded Systems. *Formal Methods in System Design*. Special issue on best papers of MEMOCODE'04, Springer. In press.

- C. Erbas, S. Cerav-Erbas, and A. D. Pimentel. Multiobjective Optimization and Evolutionary Algorithms for the Application Mapping Problem in Multiprocessor System-on-Chip Design. *IEEE Transactions on Evolutionary Computation*, 10(3):358-374, June 2006.

- A. D. Pimentel, C. Erbas, and S. Polstra. A Systematic Approach to Exploring Embedded System Architectures at Multiple Abstraction Levels, *IEEE Transactions on Computers*, 55(2):99-112, February 2006.

International conference/workshop publications

- M. Thompson, A. D. Pimentel, S. Polstra, and C. Erbas. A Mixed-level Co-simulation Technique for System-level Design Space Exploration. To appear in *Proc. of the IEEE Workshop on Embedded Systems for Real-Time Multimedia*, Seoul, Korea, Oct. 2006.

- A. D. Pimentel, M. Thompson, S. Polstra, and C. Erbas. On the Calibration of Abstract Performance Models for System-level Design Space Exploration. In *Proc. of the Int. Conference on Embedded Computer Systems: Architectures, Modeling, and Simulation*, pages 71–77, Samos, Greece, July 2006.

- C. Erbas, S. Cerav-Erbas, and A. D. Pimentel. Static Priority Scheduling of Event-Triggered Real-Time Embedded Systems. In *Proc. of the International Conference on Formal Methods and Models for Codesign*, pages 109–118, San Diego, USA, June 2004.

- C. Erbas, S. Cerav-Erbas, and A. D. Pimentel. A Multiobjective Optimization Model for Exploring Multiprocessor Mappings of Process Networks. In *Proc. of the International Conference on Hardware/Software Codesign and System Synthesis*, pages 182–187, Newport Beach, USA, Oct. 2003.

- C. Erbas and A. D. Pimentel. Utilizing Synthesis Methods in Accurate System-level Exploration of Heterogeneous Embedded Systems. In *Proc. of the IEEE Workshop on Signal Processing Systems*, pages 310–315, Seoul, Korea, August 27-29, Aug. 2003.

- C. Erbas, S. Polstra, and A. D. Pimentel. IDF Models for Trace Transformations: A Case Study in Computational Refinement. In A. Pimentel and S. Vassiliadis (eds), *Computer Systems: Architectures, Modeling, and Simulation*, LNCS vol. 3133, Springer, pages 178–187, 2004.

- A. D. Pimentel and C. Erbas. An IDF-based Trace Transformation Method for Communication Refinement. In *Proc. of the Design Automation Conference*, pages 402–407, Anaheim, USA, June 2003.

Biography

Çağkan Erbaş was born on 8 February 1976 in Kütahya, Turkey. He grew up in İzmir, where he obtained his highschool diploma from İzmir Fen Lisesi. After highschool, he attended Middle East Technical University in Ankara to study electrical engineering. He graduated from the university in 1998 and worked for a short period at Aselsan. In 1999, he moved back to İzmir and worked at Türkiye İş Bankası until 2001. During this period, he also attended the computer engineering masters program at Ege University. In 2001, he moved to Frankfurt, Germany to work for Accenture. After obtaining his masters degree in 2002, Çağkan moved to Amsterdam and started working towards his PhD degree at the University of Amsterdam. Under the supervision of Dr. Andy Pimentel, he has performed the work described in this thesis during the period from 2002 to 2006. He is currently working as a researcher at the University of Amsterdam.

www.ingramcontent.com/pod-product-compliance
Ingram Content Group UK Ltd.
Pitfield, Milton Keynes, MK11 3LW, UK
UKHW021608110926
15112UKWH00017B/126

9 789056 294557